VIENNA

D0906022

- A in the text denotes a highly recommended sight
- A complete A–Z of practical information starts on p. 113
- Extensive mapping on cover flaps

Printed in Switzerland by Weber SA, Bienne.

2nd edition
Reprinted with corrections 1996

Although we make every effort to ensure the accuracy of the information in this guide, changes do occur. If you have any new information, suggestions or corrections to contribute, we would like to hear from you. Please write to Berlitz Publishing at one of the above addresses.

Text:	Jack Altman
Editor:	Tanya Colbourne
Photography:	Jon Davison, Jean-Claude Vieilleford (pp. 28, 62, 80, 84, 92, 94, 96), Lichtbildstelle BMLF, Wien (p. 43)
Layout:	Visual Image
Cartography:	🌐 Falk-Verlag
Thanks to:	Romana Fullerney of Berlitz Vienna.

Cover photo: *Schönbrunn* © Telegraph Colour Library

CONTENTS

Vienna and the Viennese

Vienna has always been a city of romance and legend. Part of the adventure of going there is discovering how much is true, how much fantasy.

Are the Viennese really so elegant and worldly as they say? Do they still waltz to the music of Strauss? Do those horses at the Spanish Riding School actually walk on air? Do the taxi drivers really hum a few bars of *The Magic Flute* as they drive you to the opera? Does the Sachertorte chocolate cake literally melt in your mouth? Can that violin in the Heurigen wine garden really move a bank manager to tears?

The answer to this kind of question is both yes and no. Romance and reality intermingle in Vienna. Even the 'Blue' Danube is brown for the most part, except for a small section siphoned off through Donaupark, which is as blue as the waltz promised us. Nothing in Vienna is straightforward!

East-West Crossroads

Historically, Vienna has always been a crossroads of eastern and western European civilization. According to the wily 19th-century statesman Metternich, the Balkans begin at the Rennweg, a busy shopping street leading eastwards from the centre of town.

A melting pot long before New York, Vienna has perpetually defied a simple national label. As capital of the Habsburg empire, Vienna was home not only to Slavs and Hungarians, but also to Germans, Spaniards, Italians and Flemings. Its language is German – with a distinctive Viennese touch – but the city and the people obviously have too much Balkan and Latin in them to be grouped with Hamburg, Berlin or Frankfurt. The wind that sweeps down the Landstrasse has the unmistakable bite of the steppes, but by the time it reaches the centre of town, as often as not, it's been tamed by a warm breeze from the south. At the foot of the lofty Stephansdom **5**

(St Stephen's Cathedral) you feel yourself squarely in a northern, Gothic tradition. But if you go up the bell tower and look west to the city's vineyards on the slopes of the Wienerwald (the Vienna Woods), the dreamy panorama can persuade you it's time for a leisurely siesta.

Palaces and Cafés

Much of the town's 18th-century charm and 19th-century pomp have withstood the onslaught of World War II bombs, post-war building speculation and the inevitable pollution of modern traffic. Its tree-lined Ringstrasse encircling the Innere Stadt (Inner City, i.e. the First District) compares favourably with the airy sweep of Parisian boulevards. In every sense the heart of the city, the Innere Stadt is a conglomerate of baroque palaces, elegant shops, coffee shops, the famous Burgtheater and Staatsoper and a maze of narrow medieval streets winding around Stephansdom (St Stephen's cathedral).

Outside the Ringstrasse, the city sprawls through 22 other districts with parks and even farms and vineyards inside the city limits. Vienna is a city with plenty of space to relax. Its rural setting induces a more

Vienna, the city of music.

easy-going attitude to life than that normally found in modern cities of comparable size.

This pleasant atmosphere always comes as a surprise to visitors. The Viennese still seem to have time for the courtesies of the old days. Shopkeepers like to call their regular customers by aristocratic titles that, constitutionally, should have disappeared 60 years ago. Failing that, they will at least address you with a nicely inflated professional title.

Music, Music Everywhere

If ladies' hands are not kissed as often as they used to be, the intention is still announced '*Küss die Hand, gnädige Frau*' (I kiss your hand, gracious lady) – with a gesture and a lilt in the voice that remind you that Vienna has remained the city of music. Here, incidents at the opera or personnel changes at the philharmonic orchestra make front-page news. Tenors, sopranos and **7** conductors have the star-status of film actors, and the hall porter will tell you whether this year's *Don Giovanni* measures up to his favourite of a few years back. It's hard to say whether Vienna is like that because Mozart, Beethoven and Mahler chose to live here, or, conversely, whether they chose to live here because Vienna is like that.

Today the city is proud of its social progress, its strong trade unions and prosperous middle class. It has come to terms with its modest role in world events – perhaps even with a sense of relief. But the past continues to haunt the Viennese consciousness, accounting for an occasional wistful but smiling melancholy. Nostalgia is a permanent Viennese trait – even today some traditionalists still regret the passing of the Habsburg dynasty. But when the Habsburgs first appeared on the scene 700 years ago, a Viennese chronicler passionately lamented 'the good old days' of their predecessors, the Babenbergs.

Incorrigible Gemütlichkeit

Although recent social innovations by the government have been generally popular in Vienna, the people remain profoundly conservative in their values. Politically the Viennese have always been impossible to define. They cheered their Habsburg emperors and then Napoleon. They welcomed the republican experiment after World War I and then cheered Hitler.

No word better describes the ideal of Viennese life than *Gemütlichkeit*. Roughly translated, *gemütlich* means comfy and cozy – the quality that takes the rough edges off life. And the Viennese protect the *Gemütlichkeit* of their lives with their undying ironic sense of humour. Nothing is so bad that it doesn't have a good side and nothing so good that there isn't a risk somewhere. According to an old joke, 'Everything in Vienna is *gemütlich* except the wind.' 'Yes,' goes the answer, 'and the wind comes only because it's so *gemütlich* here.'

A Brief History

Vienna has been busy welcoming or trying to repel foreign visitors since the beginning of recorded time. When the Romans arrived in the 1st century AD, they found the place inhabited by very cooperative Celts who had come from Gaul 400 years earlier. The Roman soldiers, sent from Britain to defend the empire's eastern European frontiers, set up their garrison – Vindobona – in the middle of what is now the Innere Stadt (Inner City).

The Romans had their work cut out fending off invasions of the Teutons and Slavs, defending this crossroads on the River Danube, which linked western and eastern Europe. Emperor Marcus Aurelius personally led the fight against the barbarians and died in Sirmium in the year 180.

A hundred years later, another Roman emperor, Probus, stayed long enough to develop vine growing on the slopes of the Wienerwald. Today, a street in the very heart of the Heurigen wine district of Heiligenstadt, Probusgasse, honours him for this initiative.

Christianity arrived some time in the 4th century and Vienna's first church was built on the present site of the Peterskirche. The ubiquitous Attila the Hun turned up in 453, but

Memorial to composer Johann Strauss (1825–99) in the Stadtpark.

he died before implementing his plans for the conquest of Vienna. His Huns departed soon afterwards.

Others, like the Goths, Franks, Avars, Bavarians, Magyars and Slavs were more persistent, burning, plundering and pillaging their way through poor young Vienna, even in the face of Charlemagne's pacification efforts at the end of the 8th century. Then in 1156 the Babenbergs, who had succeeded a century and a half earlier in driving the Magyars out, were named hereditary dukes of Austria by the Holy Roman Emperor.

The first duke, Heinrich II Jasomirgott, set up his court around what is today the Platz am Hof. Vienna was launched into its first golden era. Art, trade and handicrafts thrived, attracting immigrant German merchants and artisans. Scottish and Irish monks on their way to Jerusalem stopped off to found the monastery of Schottenstift. The first Stephansdom was built. Vienna had become an important **10** stopover on the way to and from the Crusades. During the 13th century many new churches like the Michaelerkirche went up in Vienna, as well as several monasteries, elegant residences for the nobility along the broad new thoroughfares and a fortress on the site of the future Hofburg castle. The Innere Stadt began to take on its present shape. It was also the great era of the minstrels, the start of Vienna's long musical tradition.

But it was all too good to be true. Friedrich II, known as Friedrich der Streitbare (the Belligerent), disturbed Vienna's hard-earned peace by picking fights with his barons, seducing the burghers' wives and going off to war at the slightest provocation.

The Habsburgs Arrive

In 1246 the male line of the Babenbergs died out and the country fell to Ottokar II of Bohemia. Ottokar was popular with the Viennese. He made attractive additions to the Stephansdom and started on the Hofburg. The people did not appreciate the efforts of the new German king, Rudolf von Habsburg, to gain control of the city. They supported Ottokar, but in 1278 Rudolf triumphed.

Vienna's history for centuries thereafter was a constant confrontation between the Habsburgs' visions of grandeur and world conquest on the one hand, and the citizens' taste for the quiet life on the other. Whenever the Habsburgs went about their empire-building under Maximilian I, Karl V and Ferdinand I, Vienna was neglected.

The rulers the people liked best were the ones that preferred to stay home and build things. Rudolf der Stifter (the Founder) created the university in 1365 and turned the Romanesque Stephansdom into a Gothic structure. Friedrich III completed the work and won Rome's approval for Vienna to become a bishopric in 1469. The Viennese showed their appreciation by burying him in the cathedral. As his tomb attests, Friedrich was the one who dreamed up the grandiose motto: A.E.I.O.U. – *'Austria Est Imperare Orbi Universo'*, for which an English approximation might be 'Austria's empire is our universe'.

Hungarian king Matthias Corvinus occupied Vienna from 1485 to 1490. He's remembered for his remark: 'Let others wage war while you, happy Austria, arrange marriages. What Mars gives to others, you receive from Venus'. The reference was to the Habsburgs' knack of expanding their empire through judicious mating of their innumerable archdukes and archduchesses, a policy that was used to great advantage by Maximilian I.

Picking up where the Goths and the Magyars left off, the Turks under Suleiman the Magnificent staged a crippling eighteen-day siege of Vienna in 1529. The suburbs were devastated, but the Innere Stadt held fast and the infidels were finally forced to retreat.

During the 16th century, the Reformation made considerable inroads in Vienna, but it was **11**

*E*questrian statue of Prince Eugene of Savoy, legendary conqueror of the Turks in the 18th century.

scarcely paused to deal with the vicious plague of 1679 and another Turkish siege in 1683. The great soldier and scholar Prince Eugene of Savoy came to Vienna after his campaigns for the Habsburgs. He built the magnificent Belvedere Palace, and the Auerspergs, Schwarzenbergs and Liechtensteins followed suit on a more modest but equally elegant scale.

Karl VI, pretender to the Spanish throne, returned to Vienna more Spaniard than Austrian and brought with him the strict formality and piety of the Spanish court. He redid the 12th-century Abbey Klosterneuburg in baroque style in an attempt to create an Austrian version of El Escorial. The Karlskirche, designed on a grand scale, was originally intended to emulate St Peter's in Rome. The Hof-

Catholicism that ultimately triumphed. The city emerged as a bulwark of the Church, standing not only against the Muslim Turks but also the Protestant Swedes who launched an unsuccessful attack during the Thirty Years' War.

It was Emperor Leopold I who ushered Vienna into its glorious baroque era, a feast **12** of architecture and music that

burg underwent a magnificent expansion which included the building of the Spanish Riding School and the Imperial Library. Vienna began to vie with Versailles – and anticipated Napoleon with triumphal arches, torn down later when the Viennese got tired of them.

Maria Theresa

After this feverish construction that crowned the efforts of the male Habsburgs, those resolute empire-builders, the Viennese were delighted to be able to relax under the maternal eye of Maria Theresa (1740-80). Pious, warm and sentimental, this mother of 16 children had an unerring feel for the moods of her capital's citizens. She was an enthusiastic patron of the arts, but most of all of music. She loved to have concerts and operas performed at her newly completed Schönbrunn Palace, which she infinitely preferred to the forbiddingly austere Hofburg fortress. Her orchestra director was Christoph Gluck.

Young Joseph Haydn sang in the Vienna Boys' Choir and six-year-old Wolfgang Amadeus Mozart won Maria Theresa's heart by asking for the hand of one of her daughters. (In the event, the daughter in question, Marie-Antoinette, was destined to lose her head for somebody else.) In the following years, these three composers – Gluck, Haydn and Mozart – were to make Vienna's reputation as a city of music.

Maria Theresa lulled the Viennese into a false sense of security. Her son Joseph II (1780-90), very serious-minded and not particularly tactful, shocked them into a reluctant awareness of the revolutionary times that were coming. He rushed through a series of far-reaching reforms, making life easier for peasants, Protestants and Jews. But the conservative Viennese were not ready. They were startled to see him open up the city by tearing down the wall around the Innere Stadt, and impressed by the bureaucratic machine he installed to run the empire. **13**

People felt more secure with the cynical and not at all reform-minded Franz II, particularly following the news from France of the execution of Joseph's sister Marie-Antoinette. So disturbed were the Viennese on seeing the strange tricolour flag hoisted by the new envoy of the French republic, they promptly tore it to shreds – along with diplomatic relations between Austria and France.

The Viennese were less bumptious when Napoleon's armies arrived in November 1805 and the French emperor moved into Maria Theresa's beloved Schönbrunn on his way to further glories at Austerlitz.

For centuries the Habsburgs' secret weapon in foreign policy had been politically astute marriages – with Maria Theresa the undisputed champion. Now, when it was a question of saving what was left of the empire, Emperor Franz did not hesitate to give his daughter Marie-Louise in marriage to his enemy Napoleon in 1810. The Viennese did not protest – anything for a quiet life.

The Congress of Vienna

The Napoleonic era ended with one of the city's most splendid moments, the Congress of Vienna in 1815, organized by Franz's crafty chancellor Metternich for the post-war carving up of Napoleon's Europe. Franz was happy to leave the diplomatic shenanigans to Metternich while he supervised a non-stop spectacle of banquets, balls and concerts – all the things the Viennese loved best. Many considered Franz to be more successful than Metternich. 'This Congress does not make progress,' said the Belgian Prince de Ligne, 'it dances'.

For the next 30 years or so the city relaxed for a quiet period of gracious living – dubbed the '*Backhendlzeit*' (roast chicken era) – an almost democratic time, with the Prater park a favourite outing for royalty and worker alike. And it was time for more music. Beethoven had became the darling of an aristocracy eager to make amends for its shameful neglect of Mozart. But in general the taste was more for the waltzes of Johann Strauss, father and son.

In 1848 Vienna got caught up in a wave of revolution that spread across Europe in support of national independence and political reform. Ferdinand, the most sweet-natured but also the most dim-witted of Habsburg emperors, exclaimed when he heard that disgruntled citizens were marching on his Hofburg, 'Are they allowed to do that?' He fled town before getting an answer. Metternich was forced out of power and the mob hanged the war minister Theodor Latour from a lamp-post before imperial troops brutally re-established order.

Ferdinand abdicated, and his deadly earnest nephew Franz Joseph took over. Grimly aware of his enormous burden, Franz Joseph concentrated throughout his 68-year reign on defending his family's interests and preserving as much of the empire as possible for as long as it could hold out. Vienna offered him a paradoxically triumphant arena in which to preside over the inevitable imperial decline. Profiting from the recent prosperity of the industrial revolution, the city enthusiastically developed the great Ringstrasse complex, with imposing residences for the new aristocracy of capitalism and residential districts for the burgeoning bourgeoisie.

The World's Fair in 1873 sang the city's praises and people travelled across Europe to see the grand new opera house, the concert halls, museums and theatres. The cultural achievements of the empire were to be consecrated in monumental form before the empire itself disappeared. Brahms, Bruckner and Mahler, Lehar and Strauss provided the music. At the Secession gallery, a group of young artists introduced a new style of art, Vienna's version of Art Nouveau, which came to be known as *Jugendstil*. Only a spoilsport like Sigmund Freud over at the university would suggest that the Viennese examine the depths of their unconscious for the seeds of **15** their darker impulses. Little wonder they were in no mood to pay attention. In the coffee houses the intellectuals clucked disapprovingly and the town waltzed on. A would-be painter named Adolf Hitler left town in disgust at this lack of seriousness, blaming the Jews and Slavs he had encountered in Vienna for the problems of the 'true Germans'.

The End of the Empire

Having lost his son Rudolf through a romantic suicide in Mayerling, and his wife Elisabeth to an assassin's knife in Geneva, Franz Joseph was stricken but fatalistic when he heard the news that his heir Archduke Franz Ferdinand had been shot dead with his wife in Sarajevo. The World War (1914-18) that followed ended the Habsburg empire and left Vienna in economic and social ruin.

Vienna lost its hinterland of Czechoslovakia, Hungary, parts of Poland, Romania and what was then Yugoslavia, on **16** which it had depended not only

for its economic prosperity but also for its cultural enrichment.

While the state opera could boast Richard Strauss as its director, and the old creative spirit re-emerged in architecturally progressive public housing like the Karl-Marx-Hof, things were not the same. The city suffered from raging and crippling inflation. Politically polarized, vicious street fighting broke out between the communists and fascists supporting the government of Engelbert Dollfuss.

In 1934 Dolfuss was assassinated by the outlawed Austrian Nazis in the chancellory on Ballhausplatz. His successor, Kurt von Schuschnigg, succeeded in crushing the putsch but was forced four years later to yield to Hitler's Anschluss (German annexation) of Austria – an idea that originally had the support of both the left and right.

On 13 March 1938 Hitler drove triumphantly along the Mariahilferstrasse, cheered by hundreds of thousands of Viennese who saw him as their saviour from the chaos of recent years. He was seen somewhat differently by the city's 180,000 Jews. The brutality of the Austrian Nazis and spite of many local citizens shocked even those who had witnessed their counterparts at work in Germany. The expulsion and extermination of the Jews left a great stain on the city and a gaping hole in the cosmopolitan culture in which the Jews had played such an important role.

But in some small measure the city's spirit survived in those war years. Joseph Bürckel, the Nazi Gauleiter overseeing Vienna, warned Goebbels that it was perhaps better to allow Vienna's satirical cabaret to continue: 'One must give more scope to Viennese humour than is usual in the

*E*questrian statue of Archduke Karl (1771–49), who defeated Napoleon at Aspern in 1809.

rest of the Reich'. What humour was left was sorely tested by the bombardments of the last year of the war, bringing heavy destruction to almost every major city monument, though the cherished Stephansdom was principally the victim of shelling by SS commandos, who then fled with all the fire-fighting equipment.

After the war, Vienna, like Berlin, was divided into four sectors, with the Innere Stadt under the joint four-power administration of the Americans, Russians, British and French. The penury was countered by stoic good humour but also a vicious black market. Austria acquired neutral status in 1955 and celebrated it in typical style with the simultaneous re-opening of the Staatsoper and Burgtheater, restored from their wartime ruins. Fitting riposte to the last opera performed in 1944, Wagner's Götterdämmerung (Twilight of the Gods), the new opera house opened with Beethoven's Fidelio, a paean to liberation.

As capital of neutral Austria, Vienna was an appropriate city to host world organizations such as the International Atomic Energy Agency, the United Nations Industrial Development Organization and OPEC (Organization of Petroleum Exporting Countries). With the status of a world statesman, Chancellor Bruno Kreisky even gave the city a familiar old whiff of international power-brokering. Kurt Waldheim served two terms as UN Secretary General before becoming president of the republic in 1986, despite protests against his German army activities in the Balkans during World War II.

In the 1990s, with Eastern Europe freed of its subservience to the defunct Soviet Union, 'neutrality' is now a dead letter, and Vienna can play a more active role as a pole of attraction for East and West. While Hungarians, Slovaks, Czechs, Croats, Slovenes and Poles flock back to what was once their imperial capital, Austria's position in Western Europe is being redefined since it joined the European Union in January 1995.

What to See

Vienna offers an enormous wealth of historic places to visit. Since much of the city's past has been crammed into a relatively small area, you will inevitably find yourself spending the greater part of your visit within the medieval Innere Stadt (Inner City) and around the Ringstrasse. The Stephansdom (St Stephen's Cathedral), the Hofburg (Imperial Palace), the Burgtheater (National Theatre), Mozart's house and the Staatsoper (State Opera) are all located in this area.

Although the city has both a tram and a subway system (the

For a romantic introduction to Vienna, take a tour in a horse-drawn Fiaker. In business since the 17th century, the drivers will show you the sights with a fund of amusing anecdotes and tales.

U-Bahn), the most practical way to visit the area inside the Ringstrasse is on foot. If you want a more romantic introduction to the town, a Fiaker tour is the way to go. You'll find a fleet of horse carriages waiting to show you the sights at a number of spots around the Innere Stadt, including Stephansplatz, Albertinaplatz and Heldenplatz.

There are numerous other important landmarks beyond the Innere Stadt's ancient precincts. The Kunsthistorisches Museum (the Museum of Fine Arts), Belvedere, Karlskirche, Beethoven's Heiligenstadt, the abbey of Klosterneuberg to the north, and the Wienerwald (Vienna Woods) all deserve a visit if time permits.

The medieval spire of Stephandom (St Stephen's Cathedral) has dominated the city's skyline since the 14th century.

Innere Stadt

STEPHANSDOM

It's unthinkable to start a tour of Vienna anywhere else but at the Stephansdom (St Stephen's Cathedral). Never was a monument more magnetic. Whichever way you choose to walk through the Innere Stadt you seem inevitably to end up at the cathedral. For over eight centuries the Stephansdom has watched over Vienna, weathering city fires, Turkish cannonballs and German and Russian shells.

The best views of the cathedral are from the Stock-im-Eisen-Platz, either at ground level or from the top-floor café in the Haas-Haus (see p. 79). From here you can admire the western façade, with its massive main portal (Riesentor), flanked by two Romanesque towers (Heidentürme). Beyond that is the steeple, which the Viennese, with their taste for cozy diminutives, call the *alte Steffl*. 137 metres high (449 ft), the

Steffl has an **observation platform** at the top. The view on a clear day extends as far as the Czech Republic to the northeast and the Semmering Alps to the southwest.

The Riesentor (Giant's Gate) takes its name from a huge bone found during construction in the 13th century, which was thought to be the shin of a giant drowned in Noah's flood. The bone hung on the door until the Age of Enlightenment, when scientists concluded it was the tibia of a mammoth.

With its Romanesque western façade, Gothic tower and Baroque altars, the cathedral is a marvellous example of the Viennese genius for harmonious compromise, melding the austerity, dignity and exuberance of several great architectural styles. The Romanesque origins are visible in the Heidentürme and statuary depicting, among others, a griffin and Samson fighting a lion. Above the entrance are figures of Christ and the apostles and a veritable menagerie of dragons, **21** lions, reptiles and birds representing the evil spirits to be exorcized by the sanctity of the church.

Its transformation into the Gothic structure we see today was carried out mainly in the 14th and 15th centuries. To support their petition to have Vienna made a bishopric, the Habsburgs hoped to impress the pope by adding a second tower to match the great tower built in 1433. But the city fathers insisted the money would be better spent on strengthening the town's fortifications against the Turks and the Reformation forces. As a result, the north tower was never properly completed. Instead it was topped off in 1578 with a somewhat frivolous Renaissance cupola. Yet part of the Stephandom's charm derives from its asymmetry, with one steeple set to the side.

From atop the north tower (by express lift), you have a fine view of the city. Look out for the 20-ton **Pummerin bell**, a recast version of the one made from the bronze of Turk-

ish cannons captured after the 1683 siege, but destroyed by Allied bombing in 1945. It is rung only on ceremonial occasions such as New Year's Eve.

Inside the church in the centre aisle is the charming carved Gothic **pulpit** of Master Anton Pilgram. At the head of the spiral staircase the sculptor has placed the figures of Augustine, Gregory, Jerome and Ambrose, Fathers of the Church. He also defied the medieval tradition of anonymity with a sculpture of himself looking through a window under the staircase. Pilgram pops up again at the foot of his other contribution to the church, the elaborate stone organ-base against the wall of the north aisle.

On the left side of the high altar is the carved wooden **Wiener Neustädter Altar**. On the right side is the impressive marble **tomb** of Emperor Friedrich III (died 1496), honoured by the Viennese as the man who had the city made a bishopric, and as the inventor of the *Semmel*, the little bread roll you get with every meal.

AROUND STEPHANSDOM

If you feel ready for a break after your visit to the cathedral, then walk up the Rotenturmstrasse to one of the outdoor cafés on Lugeck, a pleasant little square where they used to hang burglars some 300 years ago. From there, wander over to the Fleischmarkt; at number 11 you'll find the oldest tavern in Vienna, the **Griechenbeisl**, famous for its associations with Beethoven, Schubert, Wagner and Strauss.

From here walk around the corner to the Grashofgasse and across the courtyard of the 17th-century **Heiligenkreuzerhof** convent. On the other side, at the Basiliskenhaus (Schönlaterngasse 7), you'll be back in the Middle Ages of superstition. Here a basilisk – half rooster, half lizard – was said to have breathed its foul poisonous fumes into the drinking water, until one day a baker's apprentice had the bright idea of holding up a mirror to the monster and scaring it to death. Next door is the former home of

composer Robert Schumann. He came from Germany to make sure the Viennese did not assign the works of Franz Schubert to oblivion.

It is a stone's throw over to the **Alte Universität** (Old University), where young Franz lived when he was a member of the Vienna Boys' Choir. The Alte Universität, founded in 1365, was closed down after student demonstrations in 1848 against the autocratic regime of Metternich. The authorities did not like having these hotheads in the Innere Stadt and moved them to academies in the outer districts. Eventually a new university was opened in 1884, safely on the outside edge of the Ring.

On the Bäckerstrasse you can see the Baroque house of the old Schmauswaberl restaurant (No. 16), which used to serve students cheap meals with leftovers from the Hofburg kitchens. The French lady of letters Madame de Staël lived at the Palais Seilern, and across the street (at No. 7) is a beautiful ivy-covered arcaded **Renaissance courtyard**, **23** one of the few still remaining in Vienna.

Cut across the busy Wollzeile to the Domgasse, important to some as the site of Vienna's first coffee house, but to most because of its association with Mozart. From 1784–1787 Wolfgang Amadeus lived in the **Figarohaus** at No. 5, now a museum devoted to the great man. In this house he wrote eleven piano concertos, one horn concerto, two quintets, four quartets, three trios, three piano sonatas, two violin sonatas and the opera *The Marriage of Figaro*.

It is a thrill for music lovers to stand in the very room where Mozart received a respectful visit from Joseph

Ceiling of the 17th-century Figarohaus on Domgasse, where Mozart composed his opera The Marriage of Figaro.

Memorial to Wolfgang Amadeus Mozart (1756–91) in the Burggarten.

Haydn and where the young Ludwig van Beethoven applied for music lessons. These were the great days. Only four years later, a few hundred yards away in musty Rauhenstein-gasse, Mozart struggled to finish *The Magic Flute* and a *Requiem* before his time ran out. He died a pauper whose coffin was blessed in an anonymous ceremony for that day's dead.

Cheer yourself up with a stroll through the **Fähnrichshof** at the corner of Blutgasse and Singerstrasse. This charming complex of artists' studios, galleries, boutiques, apartments and gardens is a triumph of urban renovation after World War II bombs left the exquisite courtyards in complete ruins.

On your way over to the city's most historic and fashionable thoroughfare, the bustling Kärntnerstrasse, stop off at the delightful little **Franziskanerplatz** to see the 18th-century fountain with a statue of Moses by Johann Martin Fischer and the ornate Baroque Franziskanerkirche. **25**

KÄRNTNERSTRASSE

The Kärntnerstrasse was once the city's main north-south thoroughfare, continuing on through Carinthia (Kärnten) to Trieste on the Adriatic. It has always been the central artery of Viennese social life, perhaps because it so neatly joins the sacred and the profane – the Stephansdom at one end and the Staatsoper at the other.

The street, which has been transformed to a traffic-free pedestrian zone, boasts many of Vienna's smartest shops. Open-air cafés are an innovation in a town not hitherto noted for its street life.

A side trip off Kärntnerstrasse to Neuer Markt takes you to the **Kaisergruft**, a 17th-century imperial burial vault beneath the church of the Capuchin Friars (Kapuzinerkirche). Most impressive among the tombs and sarcophagi of some 140 Habsburgs is the double casket of Maria Theresa and her husband, Emperor Franz I. The most recent burial was in 1989, of Zita, wife of the last Habsburg emperor,

Karl I (who abdicated in 1918 and is buried in Madeira).

Back at the Stephansdom end of Kärntnerstrasse is the **Stock-im-Eisen** (literally, 'stick set in iron') which

H ans Hollein's remarkable Haas-Haus stands next to the great Gothic cathedral of St. Stephen.

27

The extraordinary Pestsäule was donated by Emperor Leopold I as a memorial to the plague epidemic of 1679.

THE GRABEN

The **Graben** is another fashionable shopping street, famous till the end of the Habsburg empire as a coffee house rendezvous and equally infamous for the beloved 'Graben nymphs', as the local ladies of the night were known.

The broad street, now a pedestrian zone, is dominated by the startling, bulbous-shaped monument to the town's deliverance from the plague in 1679. The **Pestsäule** (Plague Column) is a rather bizarre mixture of humility before God and gruesome fascination with the disease itself. You'll find a much gayer celebration of faith just off the Graben in the **Peterskirche** (St Peter's Church), designed in 1702 by Gabriele Montani and completed 30 years later by Johann Lukas von Hildebrandt.

provides the name for the little square leading to the Graben. In the Middle Ages, journeymen locksmiths arriving in Vienna would drive a nail into the gnarled old trunk for good luck. The nails are still there.

Controversial newcomer to the square is the curving steel, glass and marble **Haas-Haus** shopping centre designed by Hans Hollein. If you go inside and up to the café you'll be rewarded with a magnificent view of the cathedral through **28** the floor to ceiling windows.

The form of the building is dictated by the graceful oval of the nave, with its rows of pews curving outwards, each decorated with three carved angels' heads. It provides a splendid example of how Viennese Baroque manages more often than not to be both sumptuous and intimate.

The domed church of St Peter (Peterskirche) was designed by Gabriele Montani in 1702.

IN AND AROUND THE JEWISH QUARTER

From here you can make your way through the old **Jewish quarter**, still in large part a garment district. The Judenplatz (Jews' Square) housed a synagogue until 1421, when it was dismantled in a pogrom and its stones carted off to build an extension to the Alte Universität. The one synagogue (out of the city's 24) to have survived the Nazis' 1938 *Kristallnacht* pogrom is at

The Ankeruhr on Hoher Markt features a midday parade of famous historical figures.

Seitenstettengasse 4. Together with a new **Jewish Museum**, it stands behind a protective block of apartment buildings next to the weird Kornhäuselturm, studio and home of 19th-century architect Josef Kornhäusel. Inside, he built a drawbridge which he could pull up when he wanted to shut himself off in his studio after a quarrel with his wife. The Judengasse leads to the city's most ancient church, the ivy-covered Romanesque **Ruprechtskirche**, built in the 12th century on the site of the 8th-century church.

Go west to Salvatorgasse, past the superb Renaissance porch of the Salvatorkapelle, a happy marriage of Italian design and Austrian late-Gothic sculpture. Beyond it is the slender jewel of 14th-century Gothic, the church of **Maria am Gestade** ('Mary on the banks'). Look out for the delicate tower, the canopied porch and the remains of Gothic stained glass in the choir.

ROMAN VIENNA

The Ruprechtskirche is near the northeast corner of the original Roman settlement, Vindobona – bounded by Rotenturmstrasse to the east, Salzgries to the north, Tiefer Graben to the west, and Naglergasse and the Graben to the south. Appropriately the Marc Aurel-Strasse, named after the Roman emperor who died in AD 180, takes you from the Ruprechtskirche to the **Hoher Markt**, an old Vienna square that began life as Vindobona's forum. A little museum (at No. 2) shows the remains of two Roman houses laid bare by a 1945 bombardment. At the eastern end of the square is a gem of high Viennese kitsch, the **Ankeruhr**, an elaborate linear clock built in 1911 by a local insurance company. Charlemagne, Prince Eugene, Maria Theresa, Joseph Haydn and others perform their act at midday.

PLATZ AM HOF

Walk back across the Judenplatz – where with any luck you may hear an open-air chamber music concert – to the spacious **Platz am Hof**, the largest square in the old part of the city. There the Babenberg dukes of Vienna, predecessors of the Habsburgs, built their fortress (on the site of No. 7) in about 1150. It was strong enough to resist enemies but sufficiently pleasant and comfortable for festivities and tournaments, such as the rollicking state reception in 1165 for German Emperor Friedrich Barbarossa.

The Mariensäule (column to Mary) was erected in 1667 to celebrate victory over Sweden's armies in the Thirty Years' War. In the southwest corner of the square, on a building that once housed the Imperial War Ministry, is a plaque to Swiss philanthropist Henry Dunant, who founded the Red Cross after witnessing the bloody Battle of Solferino in 1859. It was on a lamppost in the middle of this square that the revolutionaries of 1848 hanged the hapless War Minister Theodor Latour. At the Am Hof church, a Baroque reworking of a late-Gothic structure, the end of the Holy Roman Empire was proclaimed with fanfare in 1806. Said by historians to have been neither holy nor Roman nor an empire, it was superseded by good Kaiser Franz's *gemütlich* Austrian one.

31

AROUND HERRENGASSE

In the Bognergasse, take a look at the pretty 1907 Jugendstil façade of the Engel-Apotheke, and then retreat again into medieval Vienna through narrow cobblestoned Naglergasse. This takes you to the **Freyung** triangle, flanked by the Palais Harrach (where Joseph Haydn's mother was the family cook) and the **Schottenkirche** (Church of the Scots), founded by Scottish and Irish Benedictine monks in the 12th century.

To the south of the Freyung is Herrengasse ('Lord's Lane'), the Innere Stadt's main east-bound traffic artery, lined with imposing Baroque palaces. These buildings, dating from the 17th century to the turn of the 20th century, once belonged to the great Austrian, Hungarian, Italian and Czech families of Vienna's past – the Kinsky, the Modena, Wilczek, Pallavicini and Batthyaninow. They now serve as government offices and embassies.

Here, too, is **Palais Ferstel**, incorporating an elegant 18th-

century shopping arcade, Freyung Passage, and the restored **Café Central**, Vienna's leading coffee house in the decades before World War I (see p. 79). Upstairs, a restaurant occupies the gilded premises of the old stock exchange.

Herrengasse leads right to the **Michaelerplatz** and the Hofburg (see pp. 38–43). On the opposite side of the square, Michaelerkirche is a curious combination of styles, from late-Romanesque to Baroque. Also on Michaelerplatz (No. 5) is the architecturally revolutionary **Loos-Haus**. Built by Adolf Loos, a forerunner of the German Bauhaus movement, its austere, functional use of fine materials shocked many in 1910. In fact, Emperor Franz Joseph was so determined not to set eyes on the monstruous 'house without eyebrows' that he refused to use the Hofburg's Michaelertor exit.

St Michael's Wing of the Hofburg seen from the narrow pedestrian lane of Kohlmarkt.

The Ringstrasse

Before tackling the Hofburg, it's a good idea to go around the Ringstrasse, probably the greatest single urban achievement of Franz Joseph. This boulevard encircling the Innere Stadt was mapped out in the 1860s along the ramparts Joseph II had begun clearing 80 years prior. The project captured perfectly the energetic optimism of the times. The neo-Classical buildings bring together all the great architectural styles in a celebration of the Industrial Revolution's seemingly boundless potential.

Start your walk at the west end of the Schottenring, in front of the Votivkirche, a neo-Gothic church built after Franz Joseph survived an assassination attempt in 1853. Next to it are the university and the **Rathaus** (Town Hall). Proceed along the Innere Stadt side, past the impressive **Burgtheater** (see p. 101), a high temple of German theatre. Beyond the theatre is the lovely **Volksgarten**. Its cafés and concerts carry on a tradition that began with the café music of the Strauss family.

Opposite, you can bypass the huge Parlament, built by Theophil Hansen after a long stay in Athens, and can save till later the Naturhistorisches and Kunsthistorisches Museum (see pp. 51–5), and the Neue Burg (see p. 41). The **Burggarten**, the Hofburg's park, leads to the **Staatsoper** (State Opera). It's worth taking a guided tour here before attending a performance. The original opera house, inaugurated in 1869, was greeted with a rain of vicious criticism that drove one of the architects, Edward van der Nüll, to suicide. It was almost completely destroyed in the 1945 bombardments. The new house is very much in the neo-Classical spirit of the original structure.

On Karlsplatz, not far from the opera house, stands the huge **Karlskirche**, undoubtedly the most important of the city's Baroque churches. It was built by J. B. Fischer von Erlach for Karl VI in fulfilment of an oath made by the emperor during the plague of 1713. If possible, go at sunset for a spectacular view of the big dome across the Karlsplatz.

The church's visual impact was somewhat diminished by the building of the Ringstrasse. However, the cool sober interior remains unchanged, with a subdued marble decor and a spacious but gentle oval ground plan similar to that of the Peterskirche (see p. 29). The oval dome's splendid ceiling **frescoes** are by Johann Michael Rottmayr, the trompe-l'oeil by Gaetano Fanti. Take a look also at the lovely painting of **St Elisabeth** by Daniel Gran in the main chapel on the right.

In front of the church, a massive Henry Moore sculp-

The Staatsoper (Vienna State Opera) was built in 1861–9 under Emperor Franz Joseph.

ture provides a striking contrast. Also on the Karlsplatz is the **Stadtbahnpavillon** (Municipal Railway Pavilion) with its graceful green, gold and white motif of sunflowers and tulips. It was originally designed by Otto Wagner, who at the turn of the century led Viennese architecture away from its academic tradition through the decorative *Jugendstil* and into functional modernism. (See p. 50)

At the corner of Friedrichstrasse is the celebrated **Secession** building (1897–8). This temple of the *Jugendstil* movement was built by Wagner's student, Joseph Olbrich, to accommodate the younger generation of artists, led by Gustav Klimt, who in 1897 broke away from the conservative academies. An inscription above the door proclaims: *Der Zeit ihre Kunst, der Kunst ihre Freiheit* ('To the Age, its own Art; to Art, its own Freedom'). The dome of gilded iron laurel leaves (which has earned the building the name of 'golden cabbage') symbolizes the interdependence of art and nature. Today, it exhibits works by contemporary artists, and provides in its basement a home for Gustav Klimt's celebrated *Beethoven Frieze*, created for the Secession's exhibition of 1902.

The largest collection of Klimt's paintings – along with works of the Austrian Expressionists Schiele and Kokoschka – can be admired in the Austrian Gallery in the Upper Belvedere (see p. 56).

The domed church of St Charles Borromeo (Karlskirche), with a Henry Moore sculpture in the foreground.

37

Palaces

THE HOFBURG

Though the Habsburgs are long gone, Vienna retains an imperial aura enhanced by its palaces. The most imposing is of course the Hofburg, home of Austria's rulers since the 13th century. It covers the southwest corner of the Innere Stadt in a hopelessly untidy but awe-inspiring sprawl reminiscent of the empire itself.

The vast complex of buildings went through five major stages of construction over six centuries, and at the end here was still a large unfinished section. To follow the course of its development, start right in the middle at the **Schweizerhof**, named after the Swiss Guard that was once housed there. Here King Ottokar of Bohemia built a fortress in 1275–6 to defend himself against Rudolf von Habsburg. He wasn't successful and the Habsburgs moved in, then strengthened the fortifications to keep the unruly Viennese outside. By

the Schweizertor archway you can still see the pulleys through which the chains of the drawbridge passed. But Rudolf's son, Albrecht I, didn't feel safe here and escaped to Leopoldsberg in the Vienna Woods. For the next 250 years the fortress was used only for meetings with visiting kings and other ceremonial occasions. The **Burgkapelle** (Castle Chapel), tucked away in the northern corner of the Schweizerhof, was built in 1449. Originally Gothic, it was redone in Baroque style and then partially restored to its original form in 1802. The Wiener Sängerknaben (Vienna Boys' Choir) sing Mass here on Sundays and public holidays (except during summer holidays) at 9.15 a.m.

In 1533, having defeated the Turks four years previously, Ferdinand I felt safe enough to settle in the Hofburg, bringing his barons and bureaucrats to

The Hofburg (Imperial Palace) was the principal residence of the Habsburg emperors until 1918.

make their homes in nearby Herrengasse and Wallnerstrasse. Between 1558 and 1565 Ferdinand built the **Stallburg** (outside the main Hofburg complex on the northeast side of Reitschulgasse) as a home for his son Archduke Maximilian. It was subsequently turned into stables for the horses of the Spanish Riding School on the other side of the street. The Stallburg, with its fine three-storey arcaded courtyard, is the most important Renaissance building in Vienna.

Still in Renaissance style is Rudolf II's **Amalienburg**, built between 1575 and 1611 mostly by Italian architect Pietro Ferrabosco. It has a very pleasant trapezoid-shaped courtyard. Maria Theresa redecorated it as part of her futile effort to make the Hofburg into a cozy home, and Elisabeth, wife of Franz Joseph, lived here when she was in Vienna.

For a while the Habsburgs neglected Vienna in favour of Prague, but in the 17th century they returned and tried to make the Hofburg into a kind of Versailles. Leopold I launched the city's Baroque era with his **Leopoldinischer Trakt** (Leopold Wing) – a residence in keeping with the Habsburgs' new role as a world power. (Today the Leopoldinischer Trakt houses the Austrian presidency, a strictly honorary post.) Karl VI carried the Habsburgs' new self-confidence proudly forward with the **Reichskanzlei** (Imperial Chancellory), where Franz Joseph was later to have his apartments, the **Hofbibliothek** (the Court Library, now called the National Library) and the Winterreitschule (the Winter – i.e. Spanish – Riding School).

It was no longer necessary to call on foreign talent. Johann Bernhard Fischer von Erlach, his son Joseph Emmanuel and Johann Lukas von Hildebrandt, were among the outstanding court architects of the time. The **Josefsplatz**, a marvellously **40** harmonious Baroque square,

was designed by the Fischer von Erlachs (who built the National Library) and Jean-Nicolas Jadot (responsible for the adjoining Redoutensaal, which tragically was devastated by fire in November 1992). Inside the old library, the **Prunksaal** (Great Hall), is one of the most beautiful Baroque interiors in the world.

Just off the Josefsplatz is the church favoured by the Habsburgs for their great events, the **Augustinerkirche**. The façade of this Gothic and Baroque structure matches the library and Redoutensaal. It was here that Maria Theresa married François of Lorraine in 1736, Marie-Louise married Napoleon (in absentia) in 1810, and Franz Joseph married Elisabeth in 1854. The sung Mass at the Augustinerkirche ranks among the finest in the city. The Habsburgs' burial church is the Kapuzinerkirche over on Neuer Markt (see p.26).

Under Franz Joseph, the Hofburg expanded considerably and threatened to burst across the Ringstrasse. At one end, the Michaelerplatz wing

*T*he Neue Burg, on the southeast side of Heldenplatz, was designed by Gottfried Semper and Karl Hasenauer in 1881.

was completed. Meanwhile at the other end, in keeping with the ambitious ideas surrounding the Ringstrasse development in the last part of the 19th century, Franz Joseph (at the prompting of architect Gottfried Semper) embarked on a gigantic Kaiser forum (Emperor Forum). This was to have embraced the vast **Helden-platz** (Heroes' Square) with two crescent-shaped arms, the whole extending through triumphal arches to the Naturhistorisches and Kunsthistorisches museums. Only the first of the two crescents, the **Neue Burg**, could be undertaken before the empire collapsed. Today it houses a congress centre, several museums and reading **41** rooms for the National Library (open to all on day passes).

For an idea of the human scale of what turned into the Habsburgs' folly, you should take the 45-minute guided tour of the **imperial apartments** (Kaiserappartements); the entrance is to the left of the Hofburg rotunda coming from the Michaelerplatz. The guide will show you round the splendid Gobelin tapestries; the smoking room for the emperor's fellow officers; the enormous rococo stoves needed to heat the place; a crystal chandelier weighing half a ton; Franz Joseph's austere bedroom with its iron military cot; and Elisabeth's rooms and gymnasium where she did her daily exercises on wall-bars and climbing ropes to keep her wasp-waisted figure.

☑ THE SPANISH RIDING SCHOOL

The magnificent Baroque hall of the **Spanish Riding School** is worth visiting on architectural grounds alone. The Lipizzanner horses perform in its elegant arena throughout the year, except in January, February, July and August. Tickets must be booked at least six months in advance (write to Spanische Reitschule, Hofburg, A – 1010 Vienna).

A cheaper option is to watch the horses train. Morning exercises are held 10 a.m. –noon Tuesday–Saturday (except in mid-winter, July and August). Tickets are sold from 8.30 a.m. at the entrance, Josefsplatz, Gate 2 (reservations cannot be made).

The Lipizzaner, originally a Spanish breed, were raised at Lipica in Slovenia, not far from Trieste; since 1920 the tradition has been carried on in the Styrian town of Piber. Using methods that have not changed since the 17th century, the horses are trained to walk and dance with a delicacy that many ballet dancers would envy. Their accom-

42

Royal lipizzaner stalllions performing at the Spanish Riding School.

plishments include classical figures performed to the music of the polka, gavotte, quadrille and – needless to say! – the Viennese waltz.

Nothing can take you further away from the 20th century than the sight of these shining white horses with gold ribbons tied into their plaited manes and tails, led in by equerries wearing cocked hats, brown tailcoats edged with black silk, white buckskin breeches, sabres and riding boots. Custom demands that gentlemen take their hats off when the equerries enter, and the spectacle more than merits the gesture.

44 *The Naiad Fountain in the palace gardens of Schönbrunn.*

SCHÖNBRUNN

The affairs of the government were not something Maria Theresa ran away from, but she did prefer to handle them in the more *gemütlich* setting of Schönbrunn (accessible by tram and underground). As soon as she was settled on the throne in 1740, she moved into the palace Leopold I had started for a summer residence and which her father, Karl VI, had used for pheasant hunts.

If the Hofburg is the over-sized expression of a dynasty that outgrew itself, Schönbrunn is the smiling, serene expression of the personality of one woman. Johann Bernhard Fischer von Erlach wanted to build a 'Super Versailles', but Emperor Leopold I said no. The architect's next proposal was still too pompous for Maria Theresa's taste, so she brought in her favourite architect, Nikolaus Pacassi. He transformed Schönbrunn into an imposing edifice with warm and decorative Rococo interiors – a symbol of Maria Theresa's 'idyllic absolutism'.

To appreciate the emphasis that Schönbrunn puts on pleasure, rather than imperial pomp, it is best to visit the **gardens** first. With the exception of the Kammergarten (Chamber Garden) and Kronprinzengarten (Crown Prince Garden) to the immediate left and right of the palace, the park has always been open to the public. Maria Theresa liked to have her Viennese around her. The park, laid out in the classical French manner, is dominated by the **Gloriette**, a neo-Classical colonnade perched on the crest of a hill. It is difficult to say which view is prettier – the graceful silhouette of the Gloriette against a sunset viewed from the palace, or a bright morning view from the Gloriette over the whole of Vienna to the north and the Wienerwald to the south.

On the way to the Gloriette you will pass the Neptune Fountain and countless other statues of ancient mythology. East of the Neptune Fountain are the incredible half-buried '**Roman ruins**', built by von 45

Hohenberg in 1778, complete with fragmented Corinthian columns, friezes and archways. Nearby is the Schöner Brunnen (Beautiful Spring), discovered by Emperor Matthias around 1615, from which the palace took its name. West of Neptune is a little zoo, established in 1752 by Franz I, the consort of Maria Theresa, a topiary maze and a Tyrolean Garden (where you'll also find a café).

On your way across the courtyard to the front entrance of the palace you'll see on the right the Schlosstheater, now

the site of summer chamber opera performances. In 1908 Franz Joseph's 60th anniversary as emperor was celebrated there with a ballet that included 43 Habsburg archdukes and archduchesses aged 3 to 18.

A guided tour of the **palace** (in English) will give you a glimpse of the sumptuous coziness in which Maria Theresa and her successors handled the affairs of state: her breakfast room, decorated with the needlework of the empress and her myriad daughters; the **Spiegelsaal** (Hall of Mirrors) in which the young Mozart gave his first royal recital; the **Chinesisches Rundkabinett** (Chinese Round Room), also known as Maria Theresa's Konspirationstafelstube (which roughly translated means 'top secret dining room'). When she met here for secret consultations, a table rose from the floor with a completely prepared dinner so that no servants would be present during the conversation. You can also see the billiard room in which guests could amuse themselves while awaiting an audience with Franz Joseph. He too preferred Schönbrunn to the Hofburg and kept his mistress, actress Katharina Schratt, in a villa in the neighbouring district of Hietzing. Also on view is the bedroom where he died on 30 November 1916, at the age of 86.

A panoramic view of Schönbrunn Palace and Vienna's skyline from the height of the Gloriette (above left); the Neptune Fountain at Schönbrunn (right).

You should not miss what is now known as the **Napoleon Room** (originally Maria Theresa's bedroom), where the French emperor stayed on his way to the battle of Austerlitz

and where his son, the Duke of Reichstadt, spent his last sad years. It is a moment both pathetic and awe-inspiring to sense Napoleon's presence in the room that now contains the death mask and stuffed pet bird of his son.

The dazzling luxury of the ballrooms and dining rooms, side by side with the intimacy of the living quarters, present a constant contrast of the stately and the human in the lives of the Habsburgs. It was here that the last Habsburg abdicated and Kennedy and Khrushchev met. In the adjoining **Wagenburg** museum, you can see an impressive collection of coaches used by the imperial court, including the gilded coronation car of Karl VI.

 BELVEDERE

Of all the palaces built for the princes, dukes and barons serving the Habsburgs, the most splendid is certainly the Belvedere, the summer palace of Prince Eugene of Savoy. Regarded by many as Vienna's finest flower of Baroque residential architecture, it rivals Schönbrunn and the Hofburg.

Though close to the Innere Stadt, in the 3rd District, the palace is an enchanted world apart with its mythical sculptures, fountains, waterfalls, ponds and gardens. The **Unteres** (or Lower) **Belvedere** was built by Johann Lukas von Hildebrandt in 1714–6, and served as Prince Eugene's summer residence. (His winter palace is another jewel now brightening the lives of bureaucrats in the Finance Ministry on Himmelpfortgasse.) The palace was acquired by Maria Theresa after the prince's death, and was used by various members of the Habsburg dynasty, including Archduke Franz Ferdinand prior to his assassination at Sarajevo in 1914. Today the Lower Belvedere houses the Museum of Austrian Baroque (see p. 56), while the palace's

Belvedere Palace is one of the most impressive examples of baroque architecture in the world.

Orangerie is home to the Museum of Medieval Austrian Art (see p. 56).

Prince Eugene held his banquets and other festivities in the **Oberes** (or Upper) **Belvedere**, completed in 1723. John Foster Dulles, Vyacheslav Molotov, Harold Macmillan, Antoine Pinay and Leopold Figl met here in 1955 to sign the treaty which gave Austria its independence as a neutral country. Today the Upper Belvedere is home to the Austrian Gallery of the 19th and 20th Centuries (see p. 56)

Nowhere will you get a more panoramic view of the city skyline than from the **terrace** of the Oberes (Upper) Belvedere, which has changed remarkably little since Bellotto-Canaletto painted it in 1760.

To enjoy the fairy-tale pleasures of the main gardens start at the Upper Belvedere, whose entrance is at Prinz-Eugen-Strasse 27. If possible, go to enjoy the view of the Upper Belvedere at sunset. On fine summer evenings there is a Sound and Light show.

Jugendstil – Vienna around 1900

In Austria, *Jugendstil* caught the imagination of the art world and the result was the foundation of the Secession by a group of renegade artists from the Academy in 1897. The central figure of the Secession was Gustav Klimt, whose erotic, fairy-tale-like painting and themes came to embody *Jugendstil* for many. One of the key tenets for artists like Klimt and Koloman Moser, and architects Otto Wagner and Josef Hoffmann was the linking of function and aesthetic.

Klimt's decorative elegance was a particular source of inspiration for Schiele, whose linearity and subtlety reveals the strong influence of the *Jugendstil* movement. Schiele however emphasized expression over decoration concentrating on the human figure. The expression of feelings through colours and lines was of equal importance to the Austrian painter and writer Oskar Kokoschka, a leading exponent of Expressionism.

Museums

The Austrian capital has over 120 museums and collections, ranging from the Kunsthistorisches Museum and the Albertina to the Circus and Clown Museum and the Firefighting Museum. For a comprehensive list of Vienna's museums and galleries, pick up the free *Museums* brochure from the tourist information office. (See OPENING HOURS and PLANNING YOUR BUDGET in the Blueprint section.)

KUNSTHISTORISCHES MUSEUM

If Vienna's Kunsthistorisches Museum (Museum of Fine Arts) is less well known than the Louvre or the Prado, it may simply be because the name isn't quite catchy enough. For the collection is, quite simply, magnificent. Perhaps because it has benefited from the cultural diversity of the Habsburg empire, it encompasses a much broader spectrum of Western European art than the more celebrated museums.

Since you cannot hope to see more than just the tip of the iceberg in one visit, it is probably best to concentrate on a few of the real masterpieces. Start with the Gallery of Paintings on the first floor – this covers European art from the 16th–18th century. Paintings are arranged by national school, with Dutch, Flemish, German and English works in the east wing (to the left of the main entrance), and Italian, Spanish and French paintings in the west wing.

Gallery of Paintings First Floor, East Wing

The list below represents key works by some of the greatest Dutch, Flemish and German pre-modern masters.

Pieter Brueghel the Elder (c. 1525–69). An entire room comprising nearly half of the Flemish artist's total output including popular peasant themes such as *Children's Games* and *Peasant Wedding*, or biblical subjects such as *Christ Carrying the Cross* and *Building the Tower of Babel.* **51**

*A*ntonio Canova's powerful statue of Theseus Conquering a Centaur in the Kunsthistorisches Museum (left); the museum's interior (above).

Albrecht Dürer (1471–1528). Six of the great German master's works are on display, including the celebrated *Mar-*

tyrdom of 10,000 Christians. The artist brings the same dignity to his worldly *Portrait of Emperor Maximilian I* as to his intensely spiritual *The Holy Trinity Surrounded by All Saints.*

Lucas Cranach the Elder (1472–1553). Look out for the splendid painting of a serene Judith holding the head of the Assyrian general Holophernes, whom she has just decapitated.

Hans Holbein the Younger (1497–1543). Look out for the famous tight-lipped portrait of Henry VIII's third wife, *Jane Seymour.*

Anthony Van Dyck (1599–1641). The Flemish master is represented here by the beardless *Young Field Commander.*

Peter Paul Rubens (1577–1640). No picture is more enjoyable in the extensive Rubens selection than the portrait of his fat and sassy second wife Hélène Fourment – titled *The Little Fur Coat.* Rubens' *Self-Portrait* is also on display.

Rembrandt (1606–1669). Look out for his two superb self-portraits and a portrait of the artist's mother.

Jan Vermeer (1632–1675). The celebrated *Allegory of Painting* shows the Dutch artist painting a shy young lady.

Thomas Gainsborough (1727–88). The evocative *Suffolk Landscape* is enough to make even the most unpatriotic Englishman homesick.

Jacob van Ruisdael (1628–1682). *Big Forest* serves as a soothing finale to the museum's Northern European paintings. **53**

Gallery of Paintings
First Floor, West Wing

This section is devoted primarily to Italian masters.

Titian (c. 1487–1576). The Venetian painter is represented by the majestic *Ecce Homo* of Christ before Pontius Pilate, as well as two lovely madonnas.

Giorgione (c. 1476–1510). The *Three Philosophers* is one of the few authenticated Georgiones in existence.

Jacopo Tintoretto (1518–1594). *Susanna in her Bath* is of a delightfully wistful woman performing her ablutions.

Paolo Veronese (c. 1528–1588). The Venetian master is represented by his biblical painting of the *Healing of the Haemophiliac*.

Raphael (1483–1520). Inspired by Leonardo, *Madonna Amid Greenery* is a High Renaissance masterpiece depicting the pyramid of Mary, Jesus and John.

Michelangelo Merisi da Caravaggio (1571–1610). His *Rosary Madonna* and *David with Goliath's Head* are full of vigour and immediacy.

Giovanni Battista Tiepolo (1696–1770). A magnificent portrayal of Roman history in *The Death of Brutus* and *Hannibal Recognizes the Head of his Brother*.

Diego Rodriguez da Silva Velázquez (1599–1660). His

*P*ortrait of a woman by Albrecht Dürer in the Kunsthistorisches Museum.

famous paintings of the Spanish court include the splendid *Infanta Margarita Teresa* in her blue dress, *King Philip IV* and *Queen Isabella.*

Bernardo Bellotto (1721–1780). The artist followed his uncle Canaletto's example – he even used the same name at times, producing panoramic views for the great courts of Europe. Those of Vienna include the Freyung, Neue Markt and the *City Seen from the Belvedere.*

Jacques Louis David (1748–1825). Vienna has one of the few great Davids outside the Louvre, the celebrated painting of *Napoleon Crossing the St Bernard Pass.*

Mezzanine Galleries

The lower floor of the museum contains an impressive collection of ancient Egyptian, Greek and Roman art, as well as the **Sculpture and Applied Arts Collection**, whose prized possession is Benvenuto Cellini's famous gold-enamelled **salt cellar** made for King François of France. The highlight of the **Classical Antiquities Collection** is the exquisite **Gemma Augustea**, a 1st-century onyx cameo. The **Egytian/Oriental Collection** contains, amongst other treasures, the burial chamber of Prince Kaninisut.

Second Floor Galleries

The top floor of the museum holds the **Secondary Gallery** of paintings and the **Numismatic Collection**.

NATURHISTORISCHES MUSEUM

Directly opposite the Kunsthistorisches Museum (at 1, Maria-Theresien-Platz) the Natural History Museum contains exhibits ranging from insects to dinosaurs. The vast collection derives from the private collections of Franz I of Lorraine (1708–65), husband of Maria Theresa. Some of the highlights include the 25,000-year-old figurine, *Venus of Willendorf*, a 260-pound (117 kg) giant topaz, Maria Theresa's exquisite jewel bouquet made of precious stones.

55

MUSEUMS OF THE BELVEDERE

Perhaps the Kunsthistorisches Museum achieves such a balanced presentation of European art because Austrian art is housed separately in the twin palaces of the Belvedere.

You'll find the Museum Mittelalterlicher Österreichischer Kunst (Museum of Medieval Austrian Art) in the Orangerie, the Österreichisches Barockmuseum (Museum of Austrian Baroque) in the Lower Belvedere, and Österreichische Galerie des 19. und 20. Jahrhunderts (Austrian Gallery of 19th and 20th Centuries) in the Upper Belvedere.

The Museum of Medieval Austrian Art (access through the Museum of Austrian Baroque) has fine examples of 15th-century statuary and altarpieces from the Tyrol, Salzburg, Lower Austria and Styria.

The **Museum of Austrian Baroque** presents the colourful epitome of 18th-century Vienna with warm portraits of Maria Theresa and her husband François of Lorraine. But the masterpiece is Balthasar Permoser's Apotheosis sculpture of Prince Eugene in the Hall of Mirrors. Commissioned by the prince himself, it shows Eugene as Hercules spurning Envy and trying to silence Fame's trumpet.

The Austrian Gallery of the 19th and 20th Centuries (in the upper palace, entrance at Prinz-Eugen-Strasse 27) sums up Austria's image as a declining world power, culminating in a poignant last artistic fling around 1900. If you only have time for the best, start with the magnificent collection of paintings on the second floor. Look for Gustav Klimt's *The Kiss* and a splendid study of the city's great bourgeoisie in his portrait of *Frau Bloch*. Vienna's new proletariat found its painter in Egon Schiele, especially in his anguished and poignant *The Family, The Artist's Wife* and *Death and the Maiden*. Also on display are the early Expressionist works of Oskar Kokoschka, his lyrical but profoundly psychological portraits such as *Carl Moll* and the *Portrait of Mother,* and his *Still Life with ram and hyacinth.*

On the ground floor, three rooms show the neo-Classical world of the late 18th century dissolving into the plain and simple Biedermeier life of the first half of the 19th century, Vienna's '*Backhendlzeit*'. On the first floor of the gallery the growing prosperity and self-satisfied attitudes of the times can be seen in the pompous academic style of the court favourite Hans Makart. Artistically more satisfying is the treatment of similar imperially approved themes by Anton Romako in his battle pictures of Admiral Tegetthoff and Prince Eugene.

Also on the ground floor, (recently transferred from the Neue Galerie in the Stallburg) is a small but impressive collection of Impressionist and Post-Impressionist art with paintings by Monet, Renoir, Cézanne, Van Gogh and Edvard Munch, and sculptures by Rodin, Degas and Renoir. Recent renovation work on this floor has now been completed.

GRAPHISCHE SAMMLUNG ALBERTINA

One of the world's finest collections of graphic art is housed in the Albertina (at the south end of the Hofburg at Albertinaplatz 1). Named after Maria Theresa's son-in-law, Duke Albert of Saxony-Teschen, it was founded in 1781 and now holds over 40,000 original drawings and more than one million wood and copper-plate prints.

The collection represents virtually every major artist from the 15th century to the present, including priceless works by Dürer, Leornardo da Vinci, Michelangelo, Raphael, Titian, Rembrandt, Rubens, Van Gogh, Toulouse-Lautrec, Aubrey Beardsley and George Grosz.

Facsimiles of the best-known masterpieces are on permanent display, while original drawings are exhibited in special shows, changing some six times a year, each devoted to a particular period, style or theme. Any of the drawings may be seen on request. **57**

OTHER MUSEUMS

The **Museum der Modernen Kunst** (Modern Art Museum, located in the Palais Liech-58 tenstein at 9, Fürstengasse 1) contains an impressive selection of 20th-century art; currently on display are paintings by Kandinsky, Kokoschka, Jawlensky, Klee, Max Ernst,

*T*he crib of Napoleon's son in the Schatzkammer.

René Magritte and Andy Warhol.

Another museum worth visiting is the **Akademie der Bildenden Künste** (Academy of Fine Arts) located at 1, Schillerplatz 3. Some highlights include *The Last Judgement* by Hieronymus Bosch and a Venetian series by Guardi.

Most of the vast Habsburg fortune can be seen in the Hofburg. The **Schatzkammer** (treasury), in the Schweizerhof (The Swiss Court), contains a dazzling display of the insignia of the old Holy Roman Empire. Highlights are the Imperial Crown of pure unalloyed gold set with pearls and unpolished emeralds, sapphires and rubies. First used in the year AD 962 for the coronation of Otto the Great in Rome, it moved on to Aachen and Frankfurt for crowning successors. Also on display are the sword of Charlemagne and the Holy Lance, which dates back the Merovingian kings, and is said to have pierced the body of Christ on the Cross. Other intriguing artefacts include a unicorn's horn; a 'viper tongue credenza' used to render poisoned food edible; and an agate bowl, reputed to be the Holy Grail used by Christ at the Last Supper.

To the right of the Hofburg rotunda coming from the Michaelerplatz is the **Hofsilber- und Tafelkammer** (Court Silver and China Collection). On display here are the priceless Chinese, Japanese, French Sèvres and German Meissen services amassed by the Habsburgs over six centuries of weddings and birthdays. Highlights are a 140-piece service in vermeil and a neo-Renaissance centrepiece given to Emperor Franz Joseph by Queen Victoria in 1851.

Perhaps the most Viennese collection in the Hofburg is the exquisite **Sammlung alter Musikinstrumente** (Musical Instruments Collection), in the Neue Burg's National Library. There you'll find 360 pieces of **59** great historical interest, in particular the Renaissance instruments which represent practically everything played up to the 17th century. Also on view are Haydn's harpsichord, Beethoven's piano of 1803 and an 1839 piano used by Schumann and Brahms.

More mundane but quite touching, the Wiener Strassenbahnmuseum (**Vienna Tram Museum**) highlights the development of public transport, from horse-drawn tram to modern streetcar. The museum is housed in the Erdberg depot at 3, Erdbergstrasse 109, and is open most weekends.

In the end, Vienna remains more a city of people than of objects, and there are some fascinating museums devoted to its great men.

The **Schubert Museum** (9, Nussdorferstrasse 54), the house where the composer was born on January 31 1797, has been lovingly restored.

The **Haydn Museum** (6, Haydngasse 19) is where the composer lived from 1797 till his death on 31 May 1809. His **60** two oratorios *The Creation* and *The Seasons* were conceived and written in this house.

The **Beethoven Museum** at Probusgasse 6 is where the great composer lived on several occasions, and where he composed his Fourth, Fifth and Seventh symphonies.

The **Mozart Museum** (see p. 24) is in the Figarohaus, at 1, Domgasse 5.

The best arranged of these 'personal' museums, making up for the hostility with which most Viennese received him during his lifetime, is the one devoted to the father of psychoanalysis. The **Sigmund Freud Museum**, housed in his home at 9, Berggasse 19, has become a mecca for practitioners, students and patients of psychoanalysis from all over the world. Freud lived here from 1891 until the arrival of the Nazis in 1938. A photograph in the museum shows the house draped with a swastika. All has been faithfully reconstituted by his disciples with original furniture and belongings, including his old hats, his walking stick and suitcases initialled S.F.

The Other Vienna

Beyond the Innere Stadt and outside the imperial world of the Hofburg and Schönbrunn lies the vibrant heart of everyday Vienna. Take a stroll up Mariahilferstrasse, the city's most popular shopping street, or visit Café Sperl on Gumpendorfer Strasse. Running along the Linke Wienzeile are the fruit, vegetable and meat stalls of the Naschmarkt. Notice the splendid Jugendstil façade of Majolikahaus at N⁰ 40, designed by Otto Wagner.

Equally colourful though less elegant is the whimsical Hundertwasserhaus, a hugely popular tourist attraction that was dismissed by architectural purists as a bit of a joke. This public housing complex in Kegelgasse was designed by Austria's best-known living artist, Friedensreich Hundertwasser. The undulating façades of 52 apartments are decorated with bright paintwork, tiles, ceramics and onion domes. In the nearby Weissgerberstrasse is Hundertwasser's own museum, the KunstHausWien.

PRATER PARK

Over the Aspernbrücke, cross the Danube Canal at the junction of Franz-Josefs-Kai and Stubenring. This takes you to **Prater** park, an old-fashioned amusement park featuring roller coasters, discos, shooting ranges, restaurants and beer halls. In the good old days, the Prater cafés were serenaded by the ubiquitous Strauss family and their arch-rival, Joseph Lanner.

If the Stephansdom had not already become the undisputed symbol of the city, the Prater's **Riesenrad** (giant Ferris wheel) would certainly have laid claim – especially after the famous ride of Orson Welles and Joseph Cotten in Sir Carol Reed's film *The Third Man*. Built in 1897, it is one of the oldest and largest giant Ferris wheels in the world.

Next to the Riesenrad is the terminal of the Lilliputian Railroad, which on summer weekends provides transport to the Fair Trade Grounds, the Planetarium and the Prater Museum.

61

*B*uilt in 1897, the Riesenrad in Prater park has become a revered symbol of the city.

DONAUINSEL

You'll finally reach the real River Danube along the Lassallestrasse and over the Reichsbrücke. A man-made recreation island featuring beaches, barbecue picnic areas and sports facilities, the **Donauinsel** runs 21 km (13 miles) down the middle of the river.

You may be disappointed to discover that the 'Blue Danube' is actually yellowish brown in colour. This is due to the lime content of the riverbed. Be patient and continue on the Wagramerstrasse – past the attractive modern complex of buildings forming the UNO-City (guided tours weekdays) – to the **Alte Donau** (the Old Danube). This self-contained arm of the river is closed off for sailing, fishing and bathing and is as blue as blue can be, especially on a sunny day. In the heart of the

working-class 21st and 22nd Districts, the banks are lined with beaches, marinas and neat little gardens.

The **Donaupark** links the old and new Danube. More tranquil than the Prater, it has been laid out with beautiful flower beds, an artificial lake and sports arenas. It also features a chair lift and the 252-m (827 ft) tower, **Donauturm**, (Danube Tower) whose terrace and revolving restaurant afford magnificent views. From here you can see across the city to the Wienerwald and the Abbey of Klosterneuburg and beyond.

VIENNA'S SUBURBS

You must devote a day or two to the 19th District of **Döbling**, without a doubt the most gracious and elegant of Vienna's suburbs. Stretching from the Danube Canal to the slopes of the Wienerwald, Döbling includes Sievering, Grinzing, Heiligenstadt, Nussdorf and Kahlenberg. It is dotted with villas, parks, vineyards and, of course, the ever popular Heurigen wine gardens.

63

What to See

If you do not have a car, start your tour by catching a tram in front of the Votivkirche at Schottentor, and take it to **Heiligenstadt**, the heart of Vienna's 'Beethoven country'. You may want to stop off en route in Döbling at the **Villa Wertheimstein** (Döblinger Hauptstrasse 96), a master-piece of 19th-century Bieder-meier architecture, full of period pieces, and featuring a lovely English garden. At the end of the line (Heiligenstädter Park), walk across the park, past the monument to Bee-thoven, to Pfarrplatz 2, the prettiest of the composer's many Viennese homes.

*B*eethoven's house in Heiligenstadt where the composer, almost completely deaf, wrote some of his greatest symphonies.

A Selection of Viennese Hotels and Restaurants

Recommended Hotels

Despite being a major tourist centre, Vienna does not have the seemingly unlimited supply of hotel rooms found in many European cities; standards are, however, comparable. The shortage of accommodation, particularly during peak season – Christmas and New Year, and from Easter to the end of September – does mean that booking is advisable. Reservations may be made by telephone, fax or letter, and are binding even if not confirmed in writing.

In this guide we follow the star classification system used by the Vienna Tourist Board. The categories of hotel – Hotel, Pension and Saison-Hotel – each have different requirements determining the number of stars they are awarded, which means that one category is not comparable with another even when both have the same number of stars. Hotels are grouped in price ranges, and rates given are per room per night. En-suite facilities are included in the price where applicable. Taxes and extra charges are also included in the price, unless otherwise stated, but do check when you book.

Breakfast is usually included and is generally a buffet consisting of various cold meats and cheeses, cereals, bread, rolls, jam and coffee. A traditional Austrian breakfast usually includes the famous *Guggelhupf* (a kind of sponge ring).

The whole city has excellent public transport, including a night bus service, so you can always get back to your hotel even if you do not want to take a taxi. Parking in the centre of Vienna is a problem, as only short-term parking is usually permitted. If your hotel is in the centre, the receptionist will tell you where parking is available.

Other hotels may be found in the Vienna Tourist Board's guide *Hotels & Pensionen*, which is available at tourist information offices and travel agencies.

TOP PRICE (OVER 3,000 ÖS)

Ambassador *****
Neuer Markt 5
Tel. 514 66, fax 513 29 99
A traditional Viennese hotel with a prime location on Kärntner Str. It also offers a first-rate restaurant. 106 rooms.

Bristol *****
1, Kärntnerring 1
Tel. 515 16 0, fax 515 16 55 0
One of the old-fashioned stately hotels on the Ringstrasse, the Bristol rates among the great hotels of the world. 152 rooms.

Im Palais *****
Schwarzenberg
3, Hotel im Palais Schwarzenberg Schwarzenbergplatz 9
Tel. 798 45 15, fax 798 47 14
Housed in an imposing baroque palace, this is one of Vienna's most exclusive hotels. Delightful garden and one of Vienna's finest restaurants (see p. 74). 39 rooms.

Imperial *****
1, Kärntnerring 16
Tel. 501 10 0, fax 501 10 41 0
Opened in 1873 by Emperor Franz Joseph, the Imperial is the favoured celebrity hotel in Vienna. Renowned for its cake, the Imperial Torte. 128 rooms.

Inter-Continental *****
Wien
3, Johannesgasse 28
Tel. 711 22 0, fax 713 44 89
Part of the American chain, this luxury hotel offers the full range of services. 492 rooms.

Marriott Hotel *****
1, Parkring 12a
Tel. 515 18, fax 515 18 67 36
Part of a large American chain catering for the business traveller, the Marriott is situated on the Ringstrasse opposite the Stadtpark. Built in dramatic Post-Modern style. 310 rooms.

Radisson SAS *****
Palais Hotel
1, Im Palais Henckel von Donnersmarck Parkring 16
Tel. 515 17 0, fax 512 22 16
An imperial-style hotel housed in one of the palaces on the Ringstrasse. This is one of the most expensive hotels in Vienna. 245 rooms.

Sacher *****
1, Philharmonikerstrasse 4
Tel. 514 56, fax 514 57 81 0
Vienna's most elegant and prestigious hotel is a *fin de siècle* gem. Its biggest claim to fame, though, is its chocolate cake, the Sacher Torte (see p. 74). 116 rooms.

67

EXPENSIVE (2,000 ÖS–3,000 ÖS)

Biedermeier ****
3, Landstrasse Hauptstrasse 28
Tel. 716 71 0
fax 716 71 50 3
A charming town house teeming with old-world charm. Excellent value for money. 203 rooms.

Gartenhotel ****
Glanzing
19, Glanzinggasse 23
Tel. 470 42 72 0
fax 470 42 72 14
Located in one of Vienna's smartest residential districts, this hotel is particularly welcoming to children, and has a garden where they are free to play. 18 rooms.

Hotel de France *****
1, Schottenring 3
Tel. 313 68 70
fax 319 59 69
Another of Vienna's smart Ring-strasse hotels in a convenient location for both business executive and tourist. 214 rooms.

König von ****
Ungarn
1, Schulerstrasse 10
Tel. 515 84 0, fax 515 84 8
A charming hotel dating back to the 16th century on a quiet street in the First District. 33 rooms.

Parkhotel *****
Schönbrunn
13, Hietzinger Hauptstrasse 10-20
Tel. 878 04
fax 878 04/32 20
Originally built as Emperor Franz Joseph's guesthouse, Vienna's largest hotel faces the main entrance of the Palais Schönbrunn. 434 rooms.

Renaissance *****
15, Linke Wienzeile/
Ullmannstrasse 71
Tel. 85 04 0
fax 85 04 10 0
A modern hotel near the Palais Schönbrunn. 309 rooms.

Römischer ****
Kaiser
1, Annagasse 16
Tel. 512 77 51 0
fax 512 77 51 13
A baroque house with a prime location off Kärntnerstrasse in the First District. 23 rooms.

Vienna *****
Hilton
3, Am Stadtpark
Tel. 717 00 0
fax 713 06 91
Centrally located on the north edge of the Stadtpark next door to the City Air Terminal, this is the older and larger of Vienna's two Hiltons. 600 rooms.

MEDIUM PRICE (1,500 ÖS–2,000 ÖS)

Alpha ***
9, Boltzmanngasse 8
Tel. 319 16 46
fax 319 42 16
Pleasant, modern hotel near the US embassy and the Modern Art Museum. 70 rooms.

Am ****
Stephansplatz
1, Stephansplatz 9
Tel. 534 05 0
fax 534 05 71 1
An unprepossessing building in the heart of the First District, directly opposite Stephansdom cathedral. 61 rooms.

Ananas ****
5, Rechte Wienzeile 93-95
Tel. 546 20 0
fax 545 42 42
Outside a distinctively Viennese *Jugendstil*; inside a very pleasant modern hotel. 525 rooms.

Clima ***
Cityhotel
4, Theresianumgasse 21a
Tel. 505 16 96
fax 504 35 52
This hotel is part of the same group as the Clima Villenhotel (listed below) and standards are similarly good. 39 rooms.

Clima Villenhotel *****
19, Nussberggasse 2c
Tel. 371 51 6, fax 371 39 2
A charming hotel located among the vineyards of the Wienerwald (Vienna Woods). Situated 7 km (4 miles) north of the city centre in Nussdorf. 30 rooms.

Europa ****
Neuer Markt 3
Tel. 515 94 4, fax 513 81 38
Clean, modern and in an excellent position for most pursuits in Vienna. 102 rooms.

Hotel Regina ****
9, Rooseveltplatz 15
Tel. 404 46 0, fax 408 83 92
Hotel dating from the turn of the century, situated next to Votivkirche with a large restaurant serving local specialities. 125 rooms.

K & K Palais ****
1, Rudolfsplatz 11
Tel. 533 13 53, fax 533 13 53 70
Originally the town house of the famous Katharina Schratt, actress and intimate friend of Emperor Franz Joseph. 66 rooms.

Kaiser Franz Josef ****
Appartement Residenz
19, Sieveringer Strasse 4
Tel. 327 35 00, fax 327 35 5
A pleasant, modern hotel in a residential area. 93 rooms.

69

Kaiserin Elisabeth ****

1, Weihburggasse 3
Tel. 515 26
fax 515 26 7
A 19th-century building with a typical Biedermeier interior, situated in the heart of the First District. 63 rooms.

Kaiserpark Schönbrunn ****

12, Grünbergstrasse 11
Tel. 813 86 10 0
fax 813 81 83
A pleasant and old-fashioned Viennese hotel offering a traditional atmosphere. 49 rooms.

Novotel Wien Airport ***

Flughafen Schwechat
Tel. 701 07
fax 707 32 39
A comfortable and welcoming hotel conveniently situated at a stone's throw away from the airport terminal. 180 rooms.

Savoy ***

7, Lindengasse 12
Tel. 523 46 46
fax 523 46 40
A comfortable hotel beautifully furnished with reproduction antique furniture. The Savoy is surely one of the most pleasant places to stay in. 43 rooms.

ECONOMICAL (UNDER 1,500 ÖS)

Alexander ***

9, Augasse 15
Tel. 317 15 08
fax 317 15 08/82
Extremely convenient if you intend to take trains to the north (e.g. Prague and Berlin) and to make use of public transport in general. 54 rooms.

Amarante ***

5, Matzleinsdorfer Platz 1
Tel. 544 27 43
fax 544 27 43 80
A typical 1950s Viennese building on the Margareten Gürtel (the southern ring road). Previously called Sommer, this hotel has recently been renovated. 43 rooms.

Am Brillantengrund ***

7, Bandgasse 4
Tel. 523 22 19
fax 526 13 30
Pleasantly decorated in reproduction Biedermeier. 35 rooms.

Drei Kronen ***

4, Schleifmühlgasse 25
Tel. 587 32 89
fax 587 32 89 11
Conveniently situated in the vicinity of the Naschmarkt, Vienna's best known and largest market. 41 rooms.

Ibis ***
6, Mariahilfer Gürtel 22-24
Tel. 599 98
fax 597 90 90
Clean, comfortable French hotel chain. 341 rooms.

Jäger ****
17, Hernalser Hauptstrasse 187
Tel. 486 66 20 0
fax 486 66 20 8
A 4-star hotel at an exceptionally low price, in a good shopping street. 18 rooms.

Kärntnerhof ***
1, Grashofgasse 4
Tel. 512 19 23, fax 513 22 28 33
An attractive old building in a lively area of the First District, but in a quiet cul-de-sac. 43 rooms.

Karolinenhof ***
21, Jedleseer Strasse 75
Tel. 278 78 01
fax 278 78 01 8
One of the few hotels in this part of trans-Danube Vienna. 49 rooms.

Nordbahn ***
2, Prater Strasse 72
Tel. 211 30 0
fax 211 30 72
A comfortable, middle-class hotel near Prater park. The birthplace of Max Steiner, composer of the music for *Casablanca* and *Gone with the Wind*. 80 rooms.

Papageno ***
4, Wiedner Hauptstrasse 23-25
Tel. 504 67 44, fax 504 67 44 22
A good position near the Karlsplatz. 39 rooms.

Schloss Wilhelminenberg ***
16, Savoyenstrasse 2
Tel. 485 85 03, fax 485 48 76
Once the home of the Vienna Boys' Choir, this magnificent Schloss building overlooks the whole of Vienna. 87 rooms.

Tourotel Mariahilferstrasse ***
15, Mariahilferstrasse 156
Tel. 892 33 35
fax 892 32 21 49 5
A period building on a popular shopping street. 48 rooms.

Wandl ***
1, Petersplatz 9
Tel. 534 55, fax 534 55 77
A medieval building situated in the heart of the First District – this hotel was once a monastery and then a prostitutes' dormitory. Reservations necessary. 138 rooms.

Zur Wiener Staatsoper ***
1, Krugerstrasse 11
Tel. 513 12 74, fax 513 12 74 15
A pleasant family-run hotel right by the Opera. 22 rooms.

PENSIONS (UNDER 1000 ÖS)

Pensions (i.e. guest houses) are smaller than hotels and are generally family-run establishments.

Pension Geissler ***
1, Postgasse 14
Tel. 533 28 03, fax 533 26 35
Clean and pleasant pension conveniently situated in the First District. 23 rooms.

Pension Kraml **
6, Brauergasse 5
Tel. 587 85 88
Family-run pension. Clean, comfortable and friendly. 14 rooms.

Pension Neuer Markt ****
1, Seilergasse 9
Tel. 512 23 16, fax 513 91 05
A pleasant pension situated in a lovely square. 37 rooms.

Pension Pertschy ****
1, Habsburgergasse 5
Tel. 534 49, fax 534 49 49
Highly recommended. 42 rooms.

Pension Residenz ***
1, Ebendorferstrasse 10
Tel. 406 47 86 0, fax 406 47 86 50
An excellent position between the Rathaus (town hall) and the Ringstrasse university buildings. 13 rooms.

SAISON-HOTELS (UNDER 1000 ÖS)

Rooms in these seasonal hotels are only available during the student summer holidays (which normally go from July to September); the rest of the year they serve as university hostels.

Academia **
8, Pfeilgasse 3a
Tel. 401 76 48
fax 401 76 20
A huge student hostel located in a fun area. The Academia is conveniently situated at only a short tram ride from the First District. 368 rooms.

Atlas ***
7, Lerchenfelderstrasse 1-3
Tel. 401 76 55
fax 401 76 20
This student hostel is situated in one of the most lively parts of the Austrian capital, in the vicinity of the interesting First District. 182 rooms.

Avis **
8, Pfeilgasse 4
Tel. 401 74
fax 401 76 20
Situated just opposite the Academia (listed above) and only a short walk away from a frequent tram service to the First District. 72 rooms.

Recommended Restaurants and Cafés

Eating and drinking out is a terrifically popular pastime in Vienna. It is part of Austrian culture to take the family out for lunch at the weekend, and to meet friends in *Beisln* (convivial, moderately priced pubs/restaurants) or at the *Heuriger* (wine taverns). In restaurants, the emphasis is on good company, good wine, quantity of food and price – a dramatically different approach from many other Western European cities.

When choosing a restaurant, something to bear in mind during the summer months is whether you can sit outside in a garden or *Schanigarten* (tables on the pavement sheltered from the sun by sunshades). On hot summer days the smoky atmosphere of *Beisln* and cafés can be almost unbearable.

If you're simply after a quick snack, then look out for a *Würstelstand*, a small kiosk selling sausages and other local specialities, such as *Leberkäsesemmel*. These kiosks are to be found on street corners all over the city.

A recent, but by no means exhaustive guide to Viennese restaurants lists nearly 4,000 restaurants, *Beisln*, cafés, etc, so what follows is a comparatively limited selection. Restaurants are listed alphabetically within the following price bands:

Expensive	500 ÖS–1000 ÖS
Moderate	200 ÖS–500 ÖS
Inexpensive	200 ÖS and under

Price categories are based on the cost, per person, of a dinner comprising starter, mid-priced main course and dessert (not including wine, coffee or service). *Heuriger* are listed separately on p. 78, and cafés on pp. 79–80. See also the section on Eating Out in the main part of this guide, pp. 106–112.

EXPENSIVE (500 ÖS –1000 ÖS)

Altwienerhof
15, Herklotzgasse 6
Tel. 892 60 00
Highly acclaimed Central European cuisine and one of the finest wine lists in Vienna. The chef, Rudolf Kellner, was trained at the Savoy in London and at Maxim's in Paris. Definitely worth the pilgrimage to the 15th District.

Da Conte
1, Kurrentgasse 12
Tel. 533 64 64 0
Elegant restaurant specializing in Italian cuisine. Pricey but good.

Hotel Sacher
1, Philharmonikerstrasse 4
Tel. 514 56 0
One of Vienna's top restaurants. Particularly famous for its Sacher Torte chocolate cake. (Spelt as two words to distinguish it from the Sachertorte served in lesser establishments – the Hotel Sacher claims to have invented the original recipe.)

Korso bei der Oper
1, Mahlerstrasse 2
Tel. 515 16 54 6
Haute cuisine, accompanied by piano music, in the sumptuous surroundings of the hotel Bristol.

Palais Schwarzenberg
3, Hotel im Palais Schwarzenberg Schwarzenbergplatz 9
Tel. 798 45 15 0
Housed in a baroque palace, this restaurant is truly unique with a classic interior and a view over one of the most exquisite gardens in town. Predominantly Austrian cuisine.

Steirereck
3, Rasumofskygasse 2
Tel. 713 31 68
Topnotch restaurant serving *Neue Wiener Küche* (Viennese nouvelle cuisine). *Wiener Gabelfrühstück* ('elevenses') served from 10.30 a.m. Conservatory and pavement dining.

Vier Jahreszeiten
3, Johannesgasse 28
Tel. 711 22 14 3
Housed in the Inter-Continental Wien hotel, the Vier Jahreszeiten (Four Seasons) ranks among the top five restaurants in Vienna.

Zu Den 3 Husaren
1, Weihburggasse 4
Tel. 512 10 92
Elegant restaurant serving beautifully prepared traditional Viennese cuisine. The place to go for an evening of gracious living. Interesting and varied selection of starters.

MODERATE (200 ÖS –500 ÖS)

Bodega Manchega
9, Wasserburgergasse 2
Tel. 319 65 75
If Spanish or Mexican food appeals, try some of the excellent speciality options on the menu. Good atmosphere with live music every evening.

Da Capo
1, Schulerstrasse 18
Tel. 535 55 44
If you're looking for a pizzeria located in the centre of town, this is the place to go. It serves good italian food and wine at reasonable prices.

Eckel
19, Sieveringer Strasse 46
Tel. 323 21 8
This traditional Viennese restaurant has a moderately-priced menu and serves delicious specialities. It also offers an excellent selection of Austrian wines. Very nice garden.

Gösser Bierklinik
1, Steindlgasse 4
Tel. 535 68 97
This restaurant serves excellent food and is located in a beautiful medieval building, worth a visit in its own right.

Griechenbeisl
1, Fleischmarkt 11
Tel. 533 19 41
Despite the name, neither down-market nor Greek, but a very solid restaurant with lots of atmosphere in one of Vienna's oldest houses. *Schanigarten.*

Kervansaray-Hummerbar
1, Mahlerstrasse 9
Tel. 512 88 43
Probably the best fish restaurant in town. Also serves Turkish and international cuisine.

Oswald und Kalb
1, Bäckerstrasse 14
Tel. 512 69 92
Styrian wine and food, popular with media people. Famous for its delicious beef in vinegar and Styrian pumpkin-seed oil. Well worth a visit.

Salzamt
1, Ruprechtsplatz 1
Tel. 533 53 32
A trendy bar/restaurant frequented by artists, Bohemians etc.

Schnattl
8, Lange Gasse 40
Tel. 405 34 0 0
Good food and pleasant service in an area that is fast becoming a second centre for Viennese restaurants. Excellent wine list.

75

Servitenstüberl
9, Servitengasse 7
Tel. 345 33 6
This restaurant serves traditional Viennese cuisine at affordable prices; pleasant garden.

Stadtbeisl
1, Naglergasse 21
Tel. 533 33 23
Old-fashioned interior with beautiful dark wood panelling. Large range of delicious and reasonably-priced Viennese dishes. *Schanigarten.*

Weincomptoire
1, Bäckerstrasse 6
Tel. 512 17 60
As well as enjoying a selection of Viennese and other specialities, you can sample over 30 different wines by the glass, and a lot more by the bottle.

Zur Goldenen Glocke
5, Kettenbrückengasse 8
Tel. 587 57 67
This restaurant serves good, traditional Viennese cuisine at moderate prices. Pleasant garden.

Zum Herkner
17, Dornbacher Strasse 123
Tel. 454 38 6
The place to go for genuine, and probably about the best, home cooking in Vienna.

INEXPENSIVE (UNDER 200 ÖS)

Achilleus
1, Köllnerhofgasse 3
Tel. 512 83 28
Tucked away in a small side street in the famous 'Bermuda Triangle' area of Vienna, this is one of the city's best Greek restaurants. Prices are reasonable and service is exceptionally friendly.

Arche Noah
1, Seitenstättengasse 2
Tel. 533 13 74
This restaurant serves extremely good Jewish cuisine and has an impressive selection of kosher dishes on the menu.

Bier-Oase
9, Liechtensteinstrasse 108
Tel. 319 75 51
This restaurant serves good Viennese food and offers around 120 types of beer. *Schanigarten.*

Brezelg'wölb
1, Ledererhof 9
Tel. 533 88 11
A good selection of Austrian specialities is served in this former baker's shop with baroque decor. Romantic candlelight and sturdy old wooden tables and benches add to the exquisite old-world atmosphere.

Figlmüller

1, Wollzeile 5
Tel. 512 61 77
Viennese through and through, Figlmüller is extremely proud of its *Wienerschnitzel*s, said to be the largest in town. Hugely popular, and reservations are strongly recommended.

Fischerhaus

19, Höhenstrasse
Tel. 44 13 20
Highly recommended restaurant located in rural surroundings with a magnificent view over Vienna. It also features a little wine museum. No public transport.

Häuserl am Stoan

19, Zierleitengasse 42a
(Höhenstrasse)
Tel. 440 13 77
Basic, but nevertheless very romantic inn overlooking Vienna. Generous portions of succulent food at very reasonable prices. Charming garden. No public transport.

Lucky Chinese

1, Kärntnerstrasse 24
Tel. 512 34 28
If you are looking for delicious Szechuan and Peking specialities, then this is the place for you. Probably one of the best Chinese restaurants in Vienna.

Palatschinkenkuchl

1, Köllnerhofgasse 4
Tel. 512 31 05
Unpretentious, studenty atmosphere. Serves a variety of sweet and savoury pancakes.

Shalimar

6, Schmalzhofgasse 11
Tel. 596 43 17
Excellent, if pricey, Indian restaurant. Vienna has only about a dozen Indian and Pakistani restaurants; this is one of the best.

Trzesniewski

1, Dorotheergasse 1
Tel. 512 32 91
Vienna's most famous sandwich bar, despite the uninviting exterior and unpronounceable name.

Waldschenke Staar

Mauerbach. Hainbuch 1
Tel. (02273) 73 88
Heurigen-type restaurant with lots of atmosphere (open fireplace etc.). Crowded at weekends, so reservations are advisable.

Zur Stadt Paris (Blauensteiner)

8, Lenaugasse 1
Tel. 405 14 67
Basic but reasonable restaurant. Probably one of the best examples of a traditional Viennese eating house. *Schanigarten*.

77

HEURIGER

10er Marie
16, Ottakringer Strasse 224
Tel. 409 46 47
A very old, very famous and now very fashionable *Heuriger*. Popular hang-out amongst Viennese VIPs. Full menu.

Altes Presshaus
19, Cobenzlgasse 15
Tel. 322 39 3
An old and very pretty *Heuriger* in picturesque Grinzing.

Buschenschank Huber
18, Pötzleinsdorfer Strasse 97
Tel. 479 53 32
Very large garden and lots of rooms. Good buffet.

Diem'as Buschenschank
19, Kahlenberger Strasse 1
Tel. 374 95 9
A very pleasant *Heuriger* with lots of small cozy rooms. Almost always crowded.

Passauerhof
19, Cobenzlgasse 9. Tel. 326 34 5
One of the most impressive buildings in Grinzing. Full menu.

Zimmermann
19, Armbrustergasse 5
Tel. 372 21 10
Charming old farmhouse.

STADTHEURIGER

Augustinerkeller
1, Augustinerstrasse 1
Tel. 533 10 26
Large and extremely lively *Stadtheuriger* in the heart of the First District. Suitable for large groups. Traditional *Heuriger* music from 6.30 p.m.

Esterhazykeller
1, Haarhof 1. Tel. 533 34 82
Hot and cold buffet, good wine and smoky atmosphere in a wine cellar next to the Esterhazy Palace.

Melker Stiftskeller
1, Schottengasse 3. Tel. 533 55 30
Massive, deep vault makes this feel like a big cave, but very good food and wine.

Urbanikeller
1, Am Hof 12. Tel. 533 91 0
Viennese cuisine in a baroque patrician house. Traditional *Heuriger* music every evening.

Zwölf-Apostel-Keller
1, Sonnenfelsgasse 3
Tel. 512 67 77
Very deep cellars. The menu is limited, but it's always very crowded regardless. Try their blackcurrant wine – delicious but extremely potent!

CAFÉS

Alt Wien
1, Bäckerstrasse 9
Tel. 512 52 22
Café bordering on *Beisl* with a deliberately decadent and dingy atmosphere. It offers an excellent and mouth-watering selection of snacks. Interesting literary clientele in the evenings.

Café Bräunerhof
1, Stallburggasse 2
Tel. 512 38 93
This traditional and typical Viennese café serves very good food. Chamber music concerts are held here at weekends between 3 and 6 p.m.

Café Central
1, Herrengasse 14
(Palais Ferstel)
Tel. 533 37 63/26
Re-established in the renovated Palais Ferstel, the famous Café Central has been beautifully re-decorated in an attempt to regain its former glory as Vienna's most important literary café. Leon Trotsky was a regular visitor, and the celebrated Austrian writer Peter Altenberg lived here, returning to the nearby Graben Hotel only to sleep! It serves good quality, if (by usual café standards) rather expensive, food.

Café Dommayer
13, Dommayergasse 1
Tel. 877 54 65
Traditional Viennese café, nice but expensive.

Café Eiles
8, Josefstädter Strasse 2
Tel. 423 41 0
Traditional Viennese café famous for its political associations: this is where the Nazis planned the murder of Dollfuss in 1939.

Café Frauenhuber
1, Himmelpfortgasse 6
Tel. 512 43 23
Vienna's oldest café and one of its prettiest. Extensive menu.

Café Haag
1, Schottengasse 2
Tel. 533 18 10
Another typically Viennese café.

Café Hawelka
1, Dorotheergasse 6
Tel. 512 82 30
The café with the greatest concentration of artists and writers. Walls are decorated with paintings by artists who couldn't afford to pay.

Café Korb
1, Tuchlauben 10
Tel. 533 72 15
Impressive selection of cakes and a good restaurant menu.

Café Landtmann

1, Dr-Karl-Lueger-Ring 4
Tel. 532 06 21

The most prestigious (and also the most expensive) of the Ringstrassen cafés, founded in 1873. This place was one of Sigmund Freud's favourite haunts, and the setting of Arthur Schnitzler's story, *Leutnant Gustl*. The Viennese come here just to be seen. Large terrace.

Café Museum

1, Friedrichstrasse 6
Tel. 586 52 02

Traditional Viennese café, designed by Adolf Loos in 1899, and now tastefully renovated. Small selection of snacks only. Literary clientele. Covered *Schanigarten*.

Café Prückel

1, Stubenring 24
Tel. 512 61 15

Fine old Viennese café on the Ringstrasse. Good choice of newspapers. Piano music from 7 to 10 p.m. on Monday, Wednesday, Friday and Sunday. Serves a full menu.

Café Schwarzenberg

1, Kärntnerring 17
Tel. 512 73 93

Excellent café serving a mouthwatering and full menu. Lively and bustling atmosphere. Outdoor terrace.

Café Sperl

6, Gumpendorfer Strasse 11
Tel. 586 41 58

A frequent haunt of Franz Lehár's, this café was originally built in 1880 and was hardly altered until its renovation in 1983. Reasonably-priced, quality food. Billiard and card tables.

Café Zartl

3, Rasumofskygasse 7
Tel. 712 55 60

Atmospheric café. Cakes and some main courses. Snooker tables. Closed in August.

DO & CO

1, Stephansplatz 12
Tel. 535 39 69

Situated on the 6th floor of the Haas-Haus, this café has a superb view of Stephansdom. Coffee and delicious cakes; no hot food.

Kleines Café

1, Franziskanerplatz 3

This very pretty café was designed by Hermann Czech and provides an excellent example of 'quiet' interior design.

Volksgarten

1, Burgring 1
Tel. 533 05 18 0

Open-air café with small but delicious selection of cakes and various other dishes.

Heiligenstadt and the other neighbourhoods of Döbling provide a vital clue to the secret of the Vienna charm. In the end Vienna is not a conventional big city, but rather a collection of villages clustered around the Innere Stadt. These villages/suburbs provide a convenient get away from what the Viennese call the *Hektik* of metropolitan life.

For a pleasant outing in the country, drive your car (or take the 38S bus from Grinzinger Allee) up to the Höhenstrasse to Kahlenberg and Leopoldsberg on the northern slopes of the Wienerwald. The route offers a breathtaking view of the city and surrounding countryside. You'll find it difficult to believe that you're still inside the city limits. If time permits, get out and walk around – the road has several inns and cafés where you can stop for a drink or a bite to eat.

Ludwig van Beethoven (*Bonn 1770 – 1827 Vienna*)

Beethoven came to Vienna at the age of 22 to take lessons with Haydn. He soon established a reputation for himself with his early piano trios and sonatas, and the Viennese aristocracy were quick to take this new genius into their homes. These were his happiest years in Vienna. He fell in love with one after another of the three Brunswick daughters. It was during this period that he wrote his 'Pathétique'and 'Moonlight' sonatas.

By 1800, deafness had set in. He moved to Heiligenstadt to be near the park's reputed waters in the desperate hope that he might find a cure. It was at Probusgasse 6, in 1802, that he wrote in his famous Heiligenstädter Testament: 'You are unjust, you who believe me hostile, obstinate and a misanthrope, or at least said I was. In fact you didn't know the secret reasons for the character traits you attributed to me. But could I tell you: "Speak louder, shout, I am deaf"?'

And yet less than a year after writing this, he finished his Second Symphony, as joyous a work as any he ever wrote.

81

Since the end of the 18th century, the heights of **Kahlenberg** have been dotted with fashionable summer homes offering what is known as *Sommerfrische* (cool summer respite from the city heat).

During two steaming hot days in July 1809, the Viennese aristocracy had a grandstand view of Napoleon's Battle of Wagram against the Austrians. Sipping cool Nussdorfer white wine, they watched the manoeuvring of 300,000 soldiers on the far side of the Danube and the slaughter of approximately 40,000 Austrians and 34,000 Frenchmen.

The Höhenstrasse goes as far as **Leopoldsberg**, the very edge of the Wienerwald and the extreme eastern point of the European Alps. On a clear day, you can see about 100 km (60 miles) eastwards from the terrace of the **Leopoldskirche** to the Carpathian mountains of Slovakia.

A short detour to the north (about 7 km/4 miles) takes you to the imposing Augustine Abbey of **Klosterneuburg**. An apocryphal story claims it was founded by Duke Leopold III of Babenberg in 1106 on the spot where his bride's lost veil was discovered by his hunting dogs. In fact its foundation is earlier, but little of the original edifice remains. Karl VI, who was very much taken with Spain, undertook expansive (and expensive) alterations in the 18th century, making it a Baroque version of the Escorial. He wanted a combination palace/church with nine domes, each topped with a crown of the House of Habsburg. Only two were completed in his lifetime: the crown of the empire on the big dome and of the Austrian archduchy on the little one. Maria Theresa had neither the desire nor the money to carry on.

The Baroque ornamentation is indeed impressive, but the whole trip is made worthwhile by the **Leopoldskapelle** with its magnificent **Verdun Altar** of 1181, containing 45 enamelled panels depicting scenes from the scriptures. Known as a *biblia pauperum*, it served as a graphic bible for the poor who could not read the stories.

Excursions

Danube Valley

One of the great attractions of Vienna is its superb setting, surrounded by enchanting countryside and within easy reach of many fascinating historic sites. If, however, your visit gives you time for only one side trip, it should unquestionably be along the Danube. The area known as the Wachau, between the historic towns of Melk and Krems, is particularly recommended.

Just an hour's drive west of Vienna, this is where the Danube Valley is at its most picturesque – by turns charming and smiling with vineyards, apricot orchards and rustic villages, and then suddenly forbidding with ruined medieval castles and rocky cliffs half hidden in mist.

You cannot wax too romantic in describing the scenery, for this is a landscape whose atmosphere is heavy with myth.

Car ferry terminal at Spitz on the Danube.

Legend has it that the Burgundy kings of the medieval German epic, the Nibelungenlied, passed this spot on route to the kingdom of the Huns. The crusaders were also supposed to have passed through here on their way to the Holy Land.

Take the Danube river steamer if you simply want to sit and dream as this mythical world passes you by (see p. 115). For a closer look at the towns and castles on the way it's best to travel around by car. The historic town of **Melk** is **83**

*M*elk abbey (left) towers high above the Danube; (above) the abbey's splendid Marble Hall.

an ideal starting point for a leisurely tour of the Danube Valley (84 km/52 miles by the Westautobahn from Vienna).

The Benedictine abbey of **Melk** (*Stift Melk*) is one of the most majestic sights along the course of the Danube, towering high above the river on a protruding rock. If it looks uncommonly like a fortress it is because its strategic position high over a bend in the river made it a favoured point of defence from the time of the Romans. The Babenberg predecessors of the Habsburgs had a palace stronghold here in the 10th century, which they handed over to the Benedictines in 1106. The monks gradually turned the sanctified fortress into a fortified sanctuary of noble proportions, gracefully enhanced by the Baroque transformations of architect Jakob Prandtauer in 1702. The abbey lies stretched along the trapezoid-shaped cliffs that line the river valley. Two towers, together with the octagonal dome and the lower Bibliothek and Marmorsaal, form a harmonious group that softens the somewhat forbidding landscape. The interior of the church is rich in reds and golds with a high altar by Antonio Beduzzi and superbly sculpted pulpit, choir and confessionals. The ceiling frescoes are by Johann Michael Rottmayr, whose work also adorns Vienna's Karlskirche.

Before crossing the river Danube, make a quick detour to the village of **Mauer** (10 km due east of Melk) to see the late-Gothic wooden altarpiece in the parish church. The work, by an anonymous local artist around 1515, depicts the adoration of the Virgin Mary with a wealth of vivid detail.

You can now return, better armed, to the paganism of the crumbling castles on the Danube. Along the north bank of the river, the Wachauer Strasse is dotted with apricot orchards and sunny vineyards, 18th-century Weinhüterhütten (vine-guard's huts) and villages teeming with Heuriger.

The village church in Melk.

85

On the opposite bank, you can see Schönbühel and the 13th-century ruins of **Burg Aggstein**. The castle was once owned by a robber baron named Jörg Scheck vom Wald, popularly known as 'Schreckenwald' (Terror of the Forest). One of his favourite exercises was to lead prisoners to his rose garden, on the edge of a sheer precipice, where they were given the choice of either starving to death or ending it quickly by jumping 53 metres (175 ft) to the rocks below.

Back on the happier north bank, visit the town of Spitz with its lovely late-Gothic **St Mauritius church**. It's known for its statues of the apostles in the 1380 organ gallery, and the Baroque painting of the *Martyrdom of St Mauritius* by Kremser Schmidt. In the village of St Michael, look for seven stone hares perched on the roof of the 16th-century church. These commemorate a particularly vicious winter when snowdrifts were said to have enabled the animals to jump clear over the church. In the village of Weissenkirchen is a fortified church (religion and war always went hand in hand in this region) which was originally surrounded by four towers, a moat, ramparts and 44 cannons to fend off the Turks.

The most romantic of these medieval towns is **Dürnstein**, famous as the site of Richard the Lion-Heart's imprisonment from 1192–93. Devastated by the Swedish army in 1645, the castle of Kuenringer is more interesting to look at from below than it is to visit. But do make a point of seeing Dürnstein's **abbey church**, a Baroque structure with a splendid carved wooden door to the abbey courtyard and an imposing statue of the resurrected Christ at the church entry.

Your journey along the Wachau will end delightfully with a visit to **Krems**, heart of the region's wine industry and historically one of the Danube Valley's most important trade centres. Today, you can enjoy its superb Gothic, Renaissance and Baroque residences on tranquil, tree-shaded squares – unspoiled by early 19th-century Biedermeier construction.

Park on the Südtiroler Platz and walk through the 15th-century Steiner Tor (town gate) with its Gothic pepperpot towers. Turn immediately left up the Schmidgasse to the Körnermarkt and the Dominikaner-kirche (Dominican Church), transformed into an important museum of medieval art. Continue round to the Pfarrplatz, dominated by the **Pfarrkirche**, a lovely church redone (1616–30) by two Italian architects and decorated with altar paintings by Franz Anton Maulpertsch and the masterful frescoes of Kremser (Martin Johann) Schmidt. The church epitomizes the town's own happy marriage of Italian and Austrian tastes.

Krems's oldest square, the Hoher Markt, boasts a masterpiece of Gothic residential architecture, the arcaded **Gozzoburg**, built around 1270. Take a stroll along the Untere Landstrasse to see the elegant Baroque façades (Nos. 41, 4 and 1) and the fine Renaissance **Rathaus** (town hall).

By now you will feel ready to avail yourself of the local 'new wine' served in one of the leafy arcaded courtyards along the Obere Landstrasse (Krems' main thoroughfare). An outstanding example of 16th-century Italian Renaissance architecture along this pedestrianized shopping street is the Gasthof Alte Post (at No. 32).

Let somebody else chauffeur you back to Vienna (90 km/56 miles on route S3).

Wienerwald

If the idea of Vienna is incomplete without the Danube, there would still be something missing if you left out the Wienerwald – and not just its northern slopes along the Höhenstrasse to Kahlenberg and Leopoldsberg. To properly appreciate the Wienerwald, you must visit the villages hidden away in the forest to the south and southwest of Vienna.

Take the Breitenfurter-strasse (behind Schönbrunn Palace) out to Perchtoldsdorf, a serene little village amid **87**

*J*ohann Strauss' mighty 'Blue Danube' is unmistakably muddy in appearance, but more than merits a cruise regardless.

heather-covered hills, vineyards and fir trees. Continue south to Burg Liechtenstein, a 'ruined castle' built in 1873 on the site of the 12th-century home of the Liechtenstein dynasty. The park is an ideal spot for a picnic. In **Mödling** you can see the 15th-century Gothic Spitalkirche (church) and the house (Hauptstrasse 79) where Beethoven worked on his *Missa Solemnis*.

Turn west along route 11 to Hinterbrühl. The picturesque old mill, Höldrichsmühle (converted into an inn), is said to be where Franz Schubert wrote songs for the miller's daughter Rosi (*'Die schöne Müllerin'*) in 1823. Actually the whole story originated in an 1864 operetta devoted to the composer's life.

The road takes you through gentle hills down to the Sattelbach Valley and the Cistercian Abbey of **Heiligenkreuz** (Holy Cross), founded by the Babenberg family in 1133. Heiligenkreuz is named after the relic of a piece of the True Cross, given to Austria by the King of Jerusalem in the 12th century and now kept in the tabernacle behind the high altar. You reach the basilica via a courtyard, which features a **Trinity Column** (Pillar of the Plague), the work of Baroque artist Giovanni Giuliani, who also designed the basilica's

*T*he crumbling remains of the 12th-century Kuenringer castle in Dürnstein, where Richard the Lion-Heart was once held prisoner. **89**

splendid choir stalls. The structure has preserved the asymmetrical Romanesque western façade, and Giuliani's elegant work on the choir does not clash with the essential simplicity of the interior, a recognized triumph of spatial harmony in late-medieval architecture. Along the south side of the basilica is a graceful 13th-century cloister with 300 red columns.

In the town churchyard you'll find a tomb bearing the inscription: *'Wie eine Blume sprosst der Mensch auf und wird gebrochen.'* ('Like

The idyllic old town of Krems was an important trading centre in the 11th century.

a flower, the human being unfolds – and is broken.') This is the grave of Mary Vetsera, the 17-year-old girl who died in 1889 at Mayerling in a dual suicide with Crown Prince Rudolf, heir to the Austro-Hungarian Empire.

In the autumn of 1888, Rudolf, the only son of Franz Joseph and Elisabeth, fell in

---

A Song for Richard

During the Crusade of 1191, the brave but cheeky English king Richard the Lion-Heart enraged Leopold V von Babenberg by replacing the Austrian flag in Acre, Palestine, with the English one. Worse than that, he prevented the Austrians from sharing in the booty. But, on his way home, though dressed as a peasant, Richard was recognized and thrown into the darkest dungeon of Dürnstein. He languished there for several years until the faithful minstrel Blondel came looking for him, singing his favourite song. Richard revealed his place of imprisonment by joining in the chorus. His ransom, 23,000 kilos of silver, was enough to finance the Holy Roman Empire's expedition to Sicily and to build a new wall around Vienna.

love with Mary, daughter of the Hungarian Countess Vetsera. But the pope refused to annul the archduke's existing marriage. Angry with the conservative politics of his father Franz Joseph and miserable with his hopeless love affair, Rudolf decided on 29 January 1889 to spirit Mary away to his hunting lodge in **Mayerling** (4 km/2.5 miles southwest of Heiligenkreuz).

In the middle of the night Rudolf shot Mary with a revolver, covered her body with flowers and sat beside her till dawn, when he shot himself through the right temple, using a mirror so as not to miss.

The scandalous event has been so enshrined in cheap romantic history and Hollywood hokum that it comes almost as a shock to see the actual signpost outside Heiligenkreuz pointing to Mayerling, 3 km to the west. The hunting lodge where the tragedy occurred was demolished shortly thereafter, on the orders of Franz Joseph, and replaced with a Carmelite convent whose nuns keep a vow of lifelong silence. **91**

From Mayerling, drive on through the wildly romantic Helenental Valley to the spa of Baden (25 km/16 miles south of Vienna). Enjoyed by the Romans and made fashionable by Franz I in 1803, Baden became the very symbol of upright Viennese Biedermeier prosperity. Occasionally bath-

ing in the 36°C (97°F) sulphurous waters to deal with a spot of rheumatism, the gentry of Vienna built their summer villas here and wandered in the spa's **Kurpark** to the strains of Johann Strauss's waltzes.

The king of Biedermeier architecture was Josef Kornhäusel, and his neo-Classical façades set the tone for the town's cozy conformity. The best example of his work is the Ionic-porticoed Greek temple Rathaus, with Joseph Klieber's allegorical statues celebrating the ideals of the age: *Gerechtigkeit* (justice) and *Klugheit* (cleverness).

Note that Baden's wonderfully therapeutic thermal waters can still be enjoyed today in the indoor thermal pool (Brusattiplatz 4); the open-air thermal pools (Helenen Str. 19–21); and the mineral water thermal pools (Marchetti Str. 13).

Drive home via **Gumpoldskirchen**, a picturesque wine village with a lovely Gothic church, 16th-century town hall and Heurigen wine gardens.

*T*he Cistercian Abbey of Heiligenkreuz ('Holy Cross') is situated in a particularly charming corner of the Wienerwald.

To the East

The Bratislava road east from Vienna (Nr. 9) follows the Danube and traces the old Eastern European boundary of the Roman empire. Just 36 km (22 miles) along you come to the remains of **Carnuntum**. Once the capital of the Roman province of Pannonia, it has now been absorbed by the town of Petronell. In the 2nd century, under Hadrian and Marcus Aurelius, Carnuntum was a thriving commercial centre. Here Celtic timber merchants and gold-, silver- and coppersmiths lived in prosperous harmony with 6,000 Roman soldiers guarding the imperial outpost against barbarian invasion.

Stop on the right before you reach the town and walk to the amphitheatre, where spectators used to watch gladiators slaughter wild animals and each other. Today it's the site of a summer festival.

From Petronell drive 5 km (3 miles) south to **Rohrau**, the birthplace of Joseph Haydn.

A vineyard in Gumpolds-kirchen (left); the joys of this year's fruit of the vine (right).

Haydn's birthplace is now a small museum in the village of Rohrau.

You can visit his beautifully restored thatched-roof farm-house where he was born in 1732. Concerts are held regularly here during the spring and summer. Nearby is the Schloss Rohrau, the Baroque castle of the Harrach family, who were early patrons of young Haydn. The castle has a fine collection of 17th-century Spanish, Flemish and Italian art.

Continue on to one of Austria's most delightful lakes, the **Neusiedler See**. This birdwatchers' paradise teems with heron, teal, waterfowl, wild geese and egret. The water is so shallow that it's possible to wade right across – only a few spots are more than 1.5 m (5 ft) deep. If you do cross the lake make sure you're armed with your passport and a visa on the other side – the southern end of the lake belongs to Hungary. Flat-bottomed boats can be hired for fishing pike, carp and perch. In winter you can go skating and ice-sailing; in summer operettas are performed on the landing stages.

Along the lake's western shores are the villages of **Rust** and **Mörbisch**. Both are famous for the storks that favour their chimneys for nesting. Rust has nearly 50 stork nests on its rooftops! In Mörbisch, right on the Hungarian border, walk along the unspoiled shady lanes with their spotless whitewashed houses colourfully decorated with flowers and

bouquets of maize. The wine gardens here are truly idyllic.

On the way back to Vienna, pass through the Baroque town of **Eisenstadt** (52 km/32 miles southwest of Vienna), where Haydn lived and worked for many years in the service of Hungarian Prince Esterhazy. The composer is buried here.

Rust's most famous and lovingly looked after residents are the storks, who for centuries have built their nests on top of the town's chimneys.

What to Do

Entertainment

There are people who wouldn't touch opera with the end of a barge pole – until they come to Vienna. Suddenly, in an atmosphere of sheer love, enthusiasm and excitement that only the Viennese can muster, the most hardened resistance to this most challenging of musical forms just melts away. It's difficult to think of a cultural institution in another European capital that holds the privileged place of the **Staatsoper** (State Opera) in Vienna. Since this is Austria, try to make Mozart your first opera – after that

The Staatsoper (State Opera House) is a national shrine to culture.

you'll be ready to take on Wagner and even Alban Berg.

If you have tickets for a premiere or other gala performance, you should wear evening dress, though even on an ordinary night you may want to wear a dinner jacket or long dress – you'll find you won't be the only ones.

There's also first-rate opera to be heard at the **Volksoper** (Währingerstrasse 78), and operetta and ballet at the **Theater an der Wien** (Linke Wienzeile 6).

In the two principal concert halls – the **Musikverein** (Dumbastrasse 3) and the **Konzerthaus** (Lothringestrasse 20) – you can hear the Vienna Philharmonic and Vienna Symphony Orchestras, plus countless solo and chamber music recitals. You should also try to hear the celebrated Wiener Sängerknaben (Vienna Boys' Choir) who sing at Sunday Mass and other festivities in the Burgkapelle in the Hofburg.

Music in Vienna is not only that of its hallowed classical tradition, but also the joy of its waltzes – music made famous around the world by Johann Strauss and his family. It can

The Waltz

The waltz began as a heavy plodding triple-time German dance known as a *Ländler* which the Viennese transformed into a gay, whirling moment of fairyland. The man who brought the waltz to popular dance halls in 1819 was Joseph Lanner, leader of a small band. After he added a young viola player named Johann Strauss, the waltz took off in a big way. The group grew to an orchestra and Strauss broke away to form his own – Lanner sadly celebrating the occasion with his 'Trennungswalzer' (Separation Waltz).

The two conducted a prolonged 'Waltz War' for public favour in the cafés of the Prater. The rivalry ended amicably and Strauss played waltzes – adagio – at Lanner's funeral.

still be heard at concerts in the Stadtpark, in the Prater cafés and in the Wienerwald Heurigen. Or make for the *Johann Strauss* riverboat moored on the Danube Canal to listen and dance to Strauss and Lanner. The more formal version can be enjoyed at the grand winter season balls – organized by associations of doctors, lawyers, engineers, even *Fiaker* – the highlight being the Kaiserball (Emperor's Ball, without the Emperor) on New Year's Eve in the Hofburg.

The music season runs from September to June, climaxing with the **Vienna Festival** (end of May to end of June). In July and August there are excellent summer concerts in the courtyard of the Rathaus, at Schönbrunn and Belvedere palace.

The **Burgtheater** (National Theatre) is not just Vienna's proudest theatre but also one of the leading ensembles of the German-speaking world. The **Akademietheater** focuses on modern and avant-garde drama. Performances are held all year round at Vienna's English Theatre at Josefsgasse 12.

You should reserve well in advance for the Staatsoper, the Volksoper, Burgtheater, Akademietheater and Wiener Sängerknaben (Vienna Boys' Choir). (See TICKETS in the Blueprint section.)

Vienna also has its fair share of nightclubs, discos and cabarets, mostly around the Kärntnerstrasse, but the most common form of entertainment remains the sentimental violin and zither music of the Balkan restaurants, the Schrammelmusik of the Heurigen wine gardens (see p. 109) or the oompah-pah brass of the Prater.

The Burgtheater (National Theatre) is the leading dramatic institution of central Europe.

101

Sports

With a foresight that nobody gives them credit for, the Habsburgs provided modern **joggers** with the perfect route, without even leaving the Innere Stadt. Start at the Burgtheater end of the Volksgarten near the monument to Empress Elisabeth, trot past the Theseus Temple, once around the duck pond to the statue of dramatist Franz Grillparzer and then across Heldenplatz past Archduke Karl and Prince Eugene. Skirt the edge of the Neue Hofburg and whip around the Burggarten to salute the monuments to Goethe and Mozart. The entire route from Sissi to Wolfgang Amadeus and back should take you less than 30 minutes.

Cycling is another popular pastime in Vienna. Bicycles can be rented inexpensively from any one of 160 Austrian railway stations. In Vienna, the three stations that rent bicycles are Westbahnhof, Wien Nord and Floridsdorf. You can return your rented bicycle to any participating Austrian railway station. (You will need some form of photo identification.) The free *See Vienna by Bike* brochure from the tourist information office lists bicycle rental firms, and also provides regional maps of cycling routes.

Hiking along the well-marked paths of the Wienerwald is a wonderful way to see Vienna's spectacular hinterland. In the winter, these same paths can be used for cross-country skiing.

The 21-km (13-mile) beach of the new Donauinsel (see p. 63) provides outdoor **swimming**, along with facilities for **water-skiing** and **windsurfing**. For indoor swimming, try the Dianabad, near the Marienbrücke on the left bank of the Danube Canal.

You can also go **sailing** on the Alte Donau; ask for details from the Austria Yacht Club (Prinz-Eugen-Strasse 12).

Tennis and **squash** players will find dozens of courts in the Prater at Rustenschacher Allee and in the Donaupark, Kratochwjlestrasse and Eiswerkstrasse. There is a huge **bowling** alley

*V*ienna is a cyclist's paradise, with over 370 km (230 miles) of bicycle routes through low traffic zones.

in the Prater (Hauptallee 124). The Freudenau area of the Prater has an 18-hole **golf** course, **horse racing**, **horse riding** and **polo**. You can also see professional football in the Prater, home of the town's first-rate team, Austria.

Ice-skating carries on year round in the Wiener Stadthalle in the 15th District (Vogelweidplatz 14).

103

Shopping

Not surprisingly the most important shopping attraction in Vienna – a town preoccupied by its history – is **antiques**. Furniture and *objets d'art* from all over the old empire have ended up here in the little shops in the Innere Stadt around the Josefsplatz – in Augustinerstrasse, Spiegelgasse, Plankengasse and Dorotheergasse. You can still find authentic Rococo, Biedermeier and

Jugendstil pieces, including signed furniture of the great designers Michael Thonet and Josef Hoffmann.

Your best chance of finding a bargain is in the auction rooms of the **Dorotheum** (Dorotheergasse 17). This state pawnshop, popularly known as 'Tante Dorothee' was set up by Emperor Joseph I to enable the *'nouveaux pauvres'* to realize a quick return on heirlooms and possibly redeem them later during a more prosperous peri-

A *19th-century bank and shopping complex, the Palais Ferstel on Herrengasse and Freyung was built by leading historicist Heinrich Ferstel.*

od. But it was also a kind of state-sponsored clearing house for stolen art objects, where the original owners could even buy their property back if the police had not managed to run down the thieves. The items are put on display before the sale, often in the windows of a bank opposite the auction rooms. If you feel uncertain about bidding, you can hire a licensed agent to do it for you for a small fee.

Still in the realm of the past are the great speciality shops for **coin**- and **stamp**-collectors (where else could you expect to find mint-condition Bosnia-Herzegovina issues of 1914?).

The national **Augarten porcelain** workshops still turn out hand-decorated Rococo chinaware, including of course the Lipizzaner horses. **Petit-**

point embroidery is available in the form of handbags, cushions and other items with flower, folk and opera motifs. Viennese craftsmen are also noted for their ceramics, handmade dolls, enamel miniatures and costume jewellery.

You will find the more elegant shops on the Kärntnerstrasse, Graben and Kohlmarkt. Traditional Austrian costume has caught the whimsical attention of high fashion with the Dirndl, a pleated skirt with a blue or pink and white apron tied at the waist and a white full-sleeved blouse under a laced bodice. For men the heavy woollen Loden cloth makes excellent winter coats.

The Saturday morning **flea market** on the Naschmarkt is a veritable Aladdin's Cave. It is situated next to the fruit and vegetable market at the Kettenbrückengasse underground station. The market caters mainly for youthful tastes, but you'll find there's something for everyone here. Each week a different provincial town brings in its bric-a-brac and miscellaneous treasures. **105**

Eating Out

When it comes to Viennese cuisine, you must bear in mind that this city was once the centre of the old Habsburg empire of 60 million Eastern and Southern Europeans. The emperor and his archdukes and generals have gone, but not the Bohemian dumplings, the Hungarian goulash, the Polish stuffed cabbage and Serbian shashlik, and the plum, cherry and apricot brandies that accompany the Turkish coffee.

Two Viennese staples that you're likely to come across immediately are the *Wiener Schnitzel* and the *Backhendl*. The *Wiener Schnitzel* is a large, thinly sliced cutlet of veal crisply sautéed in a coating of egg and seasoned breadcrumbs. *Backhendl* is roast chicken prepared in the same way. To be authentic Viennese gourmets insist that the *Wiener Schnitzel* is served with cold potato or cucumber salad. You should also make sure that it is a cut of veal (*vom Kalb*) and not pork (*vom Schwein*), as in some of

the cheaper establishments. The *Backhendl* is sometimes served with *Geröstete* (sautéed potatoes).

Tafelspitz (boiled beef) was Emperor Franz Joseph's favourite dish, and to this day is a form of ambrosia to the Viennese. Eat it with *Kren* (horseradish) and *Schnittlauch-sauce* (chive sauce).

Another culinary delight, originally from Hungary, is goulash – beef chunks stewed in onions, garlic, paprika, tomatoes and celery. *Debreziner* sausages, *Kömenymagleves Nokedival* (caraway-seed soup with dumplings) and apple soup (apples, cloves, cinnamon, white wine, lemon juice, sugar and extra thick cream) are three more Hungarian specialities.

From the Czech Republic comes delicious Prague ham and sauerkraut soup; from Polish Galicia, roast goose served with dumplings and red cabbage; and from Serbia, the peppery barbecued *cevapcici* meatballs and *schaschlik* brochettes of lamb with onions, and green and red peppers.

Dumplings *(Knödel)*, made from flour, yeast or potatoes, are an Austrian staple served with the main course and in the soup. The *Marillenknödel* is a dessert dumpling, made of potato with a piping hot apricot inside. Another delicious dessert dumpling is the *Topfenknödel,* made with a cream cheese filling.

Hot desserts are in fact a speciality and you should also try *Buchteln* or *Wuchteln*, yeast buns often filled with plum jam, and the *Palatschinken* from Hungary, pancakes filled with jam or nuts. Finally, don't forget the *Apfelstrudel*, a flaky, almost transparent pastry filled with thinly sliced apples, raisins and cinnamon.

A violinist at a local heuriger serenades the merry-makers with nostalgic Schrammelmusik.

Finally, there's the most famous and sinfully delicious chocolate cake in the world, the *Sachertorte*. Join in the endless debate over whether or not it should be split into two layers and where the apricot jam should go.

A celebrated legal battle has at last resolved the contentious matter of who should have the right to the label 'original Sachertorte' – the venerable Hotel Sacher (on Philharmonikerstrasse) or the equally prestigious Konditorei Demel (Kohlmarkt 18). In the end the Hotel Sacher finally won, and the two-word spelling of the cake has become their official trademark. A shop on Kärntnerstrasse sells the official product in every conceivable shape and size.

*H*eurigen serve young, sparkling wine form the barrel and a buffet consisting of cold meat, cheese and salads.

WINES AND WINE GARDENS

Wine in Vienna is almost always white wine, which the Viennese drink quite happily with meat and fish alike. The best known of Austrian white wines, the *Gumpoldskirchner*, has the full body and bouquet of its southern vineyards. The Viennese give equal favour to their own *Grinzinger, Nussdorfer, Sieveringer* and *Neustifter*. From the Danube Valley, with an extra natural sparkle, come the *Kremser, Dürnsteiner* and *Langenloiser*.

Of the reds, the *Vöslauer*, produced in Bad Vöslau near Baden, and the *Kalterersee*, imported from South Tyrol (now Alto Adige in Italy) are about the best. *Blaufränkisch* and *Zweigelt* are also reliable stand-bys.

To enjoy these wines in their original state, they should be ordered *herb* (dry). Often the producers will sweeten them for the foreign palate unless you specify otherwise.

Perhaps the most pleasant thing about Viennese wine is the way in which it is drunk. The Viennese have created a splendid institution, the **Heurigen**, where you can sip white wine on mild evenings under the stars.

Wine-growers are allowed by law to sell a certain amount of their new wine – Heuriger – directly to the public. They announce the new wine by hanging out a sprig of pine over the door and a sign saying *ausg'steckt* (open). When the new wine has gone, the pine branch must be removed.

The heurigen of Grinzing are extremely popular, but the best ones are out in Nussdorf, Ober-Sievering and Neustift. Heuriger are generally open from mid-afternoon till late in the evening and at weekends for lunch. The season runs from March to October.

Beer is also a popular drink and the local *Gösser* brew presents a worthy challenge to the *Pilsner Urquell* imported from the Czech Republic.

Among the brandies you should try the Hungarian *Barack* (apricot) and Serbian *Slivovitz* (plum).

COFFEE AND THE KAFFEEHAUS

The varieties of coffee in Vienna are virtually endless, and there are names for every shade from black to white. Ask for *einen kleinen Mokka* and you'll get a small, strong black coffee and stamp yourself as someone of French or Italian taste. *Einen Kapuziner*, topped with generous dollops of cream, is already more Viennese; *einen Braunen*, with just a dash of milk, is as Viennese as can be. *Eine Melange* (pronounced 'melanksch'), a mixture of milk and coffee, is designed for sensitive stomachs; *einen Einspänner*, with whipped cream in a tall glass, is for aunts on Sundays; *einen Türkischen*, prepared semisweet in a copper pot, is for addicts of the Balkan Connection.

In the 1920s the Café Herrenhof employed waiters who would go around with a colour chart showing 20 variations of brown. You then ordered for example *'einen Dreizehner, mit Schlag'* (a 13 with cream), and satisfaction was guaranteed.

The tradition of the Viennese *Kaffeehaus* dates back to the 17th century when, so the story goes, a Hungarian opened Zum Roten Kreuz in the Domgasse with a stock of coffee beans captured from the Turks. By the time of Maria Theresa the town was full of coffee houses, fashionable and shady, where gentry and intellectuals mingled to pass the time of day. Some developed their own particular clientele – writers, artists, politicians and the like – while the most prominent cafés (the Griensteidl, Café Central or the Herrenhof) attracted all types.

For many the *Kaffeehaus* was a place to enjoy warmth and human contact rather than shiver in miserable lodgings. After a post-war lull, the institution has made a grand comeback. In the Innere Stadt, the renovated Café Central and the more sedate Griensteidl are thriving once again. The Café Hawelka, at Dorotheergasse 6, once popular with artists and antique dealers, has become a hangout for the younger crowd. Artists now prefer Alt-Wien, at Bäckerstrasse 9, and the Kleines Café, Franziskaner-platz 3, with its superb interior design by architect Hermann Czech. Intellectuals have followed the example of the late Thomas Bernhard in favouring Café Bräunerhof, at Stallburggasse 2. This café is also popular with music lovers for its weekend chamber music recitals. Chess players with a killer instinct can be seen at the Café Museum, Friedrichstrasse 6. Out in the 6th District, Café Sperl, at Gumpendorfer Strasse 11, is an elegant 100-year-old establishment with marble tables, Jugendstil chairs, an endless row of newspapers (including The Times, Le Monde and La Stampa), and billiard tables for those who really can't bear to sit and do nothing.

The legendary Café Central, nerve centre of literary Vienna at the turn of the century, has recently been renovated to its former splendour.

HELP WITH A
VIENNESE MENU

Apfelstrudel pastry filled with
apples, raisins and cinnamon

Auflauf soufflé

Backhendl chicken sauteéd in
egg and breadcrumbs

Bauernschmaus
meat served with dumplings
and sauerkraut

Beuschel
chopped offal in sauce

Blunzn black pudding

Buchteln or *Wuchteln*
yeast buns filled with
plum jam

Debreziner
spicy Hungarian sausage

Eierschwammerl mushrooms

Faschiertes minced meat

Fleischlaberl meat rissoles

Frittatensuppe
broth with sliced crepes

Gefüllte Paprika
stuffed green pepper

Germknödel yeast dumpling

Griessnockerlsuppe
semolina dumpling soup

Guglhupf Viennese cake

Gulasch Hungarian stew

Kaiserschmarrn pancake
served with fruit compote

Kalbsvögerl knuckle of veal

Knödel dumplings made from
flour, potatoes or yeast

Krenfleisch boiled pork served
with horseradish

Marillenknödel
apricot dumpling

Millirahmstrudel strudel with
sweet cheese filling

Nockerl small dumpling

Palatschinken pancakes filled
with jam or nuts

Paradeiser tomatoes

Powidl plum sauce

Ribisel red or black currants

Rostbraten grilled steak

Rotkraut red cabbage

Sachertorte chocolate cake

Schinkenfleckerl baked
noodles with chopped ham

Schwammerlsuppe
mushroom soup

Tafelspitz boiled beef

Topfenknödel dumpling with
a cream cheese filling

Topfenstrudel strudel with
cream cheese and raisins

Wiener Schnitzel fillet of veal
or pork fried in breadcrumbs

Zigeunerschnitzel Wiener
Schnitzel spiced with paprika

Zwetschkenröster
plum compote

Zwiebelrostbraten beef steak
served with fried onions

BLUEPRINT
for a
Perfect Trip

An A–Z Summary of Practical Information and Facts

> Listed after many entries is the appropriate German translation, usually in the singular, plus a number of phrases that should help you when seeking assistance.

A

ACCOMMODATION. See also RECOMMENDED HOTELS, pp. 66–72. The Vienna Tourist Board publishes an annual list of hotels, boarding houses and 'seasonal' hotels (student hostels used as hotels from July to September) with details about amenities, prices and classifications. You can pick it up, along with an excellent free city map, from the Austrian Tourist Board in your country or from travel agents. Tourist information offices in Vienna (listed on pp. 139–140) can book rooms for you – but at a cost. Telephone assistance is available from Easter to October: tel. 211 1466/7.

The homely atmosphere of boarding houses in Vienna makes them popular for longer stays. It is always advisable to book ahead, especially from Easter to the end of September, Christmas and New Year. It is also possible to stay in private homes on a bed-and-breakfast basis. This is an especially attractive option in some of the smaller villages around Vienna. A well-established bed-and-breakfast agency is: B+B Vienna, 23, Rieglgasse 47B; tel. and fax 885 219. The famous old luxury hotels around the opera are often filled up and sometimes do not accept credit cards (most other hotels do). If you do cancel your reservation, the hotel has a right to charge a cancellation fee.

a boarding house	**eine Pension**
a single/double room	**eine Einzel-/Doppelzimmer**
with/without bath (shower)	**mit/ohne Bad (Dusche)**
What's the rate per night?	**Was kostet eine Übernachtung?**

AIRPORT *(Flughafen)*

The Schwechat Airport, about 20 kilometres (11 miles) from the centre of Vienna, handles domestic and international flights. The modern building has a bank, restaurants, cafés, news and souvenir stands, a duty-free shop and the Vienna Airport Tourist Information Office (in the arrivals hall). This office can book hotel accommodation and is open 24 hours a day seven days a week. For information regarding the airport bus service see PUBLIC TRANSPORT.

B

BABYSITTERS *(Babysitter)*

Although your hotel receptionist can sometimes arrange for a sitter, there are also agencies who have a list of multilingual babysitters. A well-established agency is: Babysitter des Österreichischen Akademischen Gästedienstes, Mühlgasse 20. Tel. 587 3525. Monday to Thursday 9 a.m. to 5 p.m., Friday 9 a.m. to 3 p.m.

Can you get me a babysitter for tonight?	**Können Sie mir für heute abend einen Babysitter besorgen?**

BOAT EXCURSIONS

The DDSG-Blue Danube Schiffahrt GmbH organizes a number of trips on the Danube between the end of March and the end of October. Children up to 10 years of age travel free when accompanied by their parents, or otherwise pay 50%. The main tours are:

- 'Vienna-Hundertwasser Tour': goes from the Kunstl-Haus in Vienna past Schwedenplatz to the Nussdorfer Schleuse and back.
- Wachau: from Melk past castle Schönbühel to Spitz and back.
- Vienna-Krems-Vienna: a weekend tour especially designed for cyclists, who can take their bikes on board and relax.
- 'Lionheart Tour': from Krems past Dürnstein, Weissenkirchen and St Michael to Spitz and back.

For more information, telephone 588 000.

CAMPING

Six camping sites are located in or near the city, one of which is
open all year round (except during February):
Campingplatz der Stadt Wien, Wien West II (Tel. 914 23 14).
Other sites are:
Neue Donau (Tel./fax 220 93 10)
Wien-Rodaun (Tel. 884 15 4)
Schloss Laxenburg (Tel. (02236) 713 33)
Wien West I (Tel. 914 23 14)
Wien Süd (Tel. 865 92 18).
They are very well organized and offer many facilities.

CAR HIRE *(Autovermietung)*

You can arrange immediate hire upon arrival at Vienna's airport or
railway station. Otherwise your hotel or the yellow pages of the telephone book have the addresses of leading firms. It's usually possible
to have the car delivered to your hotel. Some firms permit the car to
be returned to another European city.

To hire a car you'll need your driving licence; minimum age is
21 years. Normally a deposit is charged when hiring a car, but holders
of major credit cards are exempt. Special weekend and weekly
unlimited mileage rates may be available.

I'd like to rent a car (for today). **Ich möchte (für heute) ein
Auto mieten**.

CHILDREN

Listed below are some suggestions for outings with the kids – which
parents, too, might appreciate for a change of pace:
- Prater amusement park features bowling alleys, riding stables,
  roller coasters, merry-go-rounds and the biggest Ferris wheel in
  Europe.
- Schönbrunn park has a zoo and coach collection (Wagenburg).

- Boating on the Alte Donau where there are kayaks, rowing boats and sailing boats for rent.
- Ice-skating on the indoor rink in the Stadthalle, Vogelweidplatz or, in the winter, on the outdoor rink at Lothringerstrasse 22 near the Inter-Continental Hotel.
- Swimming in public indoor or outdoor pools in all parts of Vienna. Look for the list in the telephone book under 'Badeanstalten' or 'Städtische Bäder'.

CLIMATE

Spring is probably Vienna's most pleasant season. Chestnut trees and white lilac are in blossom and the city's music festival is in full swing. In July and August the town's residents take their summer holidays, leaving the city relatively free for visitors, and then in September there's the opera and theatre season and the spectacular autumn colours of the Wienerwald. Even in winter Vienna can be worth the trip for a marvellous white Christmas, in spite of the cold east wind.

The following chart shows Vienna's average monthly temperatures:

	J	F	M	A	M	J	J	A	S	O	N	D
°F	30	33	40	50	58	64	68	67	61	51	41	34
°C	-1	1	5	10	15	18	20	19	16	10	5	1

CLOTHING (Kleidung)

Vienna's weather tends to be extreme – very hot in the summer and very cold in the winter – and the wind off the steppes can whip through at any time. Even in summer the evenings can be quite chilly, so you should take a cardigan and a raincoat.

The Viennese like to dress up for the theatre, concert and opera, but a dark suit or cocktail dress is nearly always appropriate. A dinner jacket (tuxedo) or evening dress is worn on special occasions, such as premieres and galas.

COMPLAINTS *(Reklamationen)*

Despite a historically lackadaisical reputation, modern Vienna is remarkably efficient. But if something should go wrong and neither you nor the famous Viennese charm can help put it right, you should report the matter to the Vienna Tourist Board, listed under TOURIST INFORMATION.

In hotels, restaurants and shops, complaints should be addressed to the manager or proprietor. For more serious affairs do not hesitate to contact the police or your consulate.

CONVERTER CHARTS

Austria uses the metric system.

Temperature

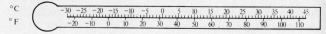

Length

Weight

grams	0	100	200	300	400	500	600	700	800	900	1 kg
ounces	0	4		8	12	1 lb	20	24	28	2 lb.	

CRIME

Compared to most parts of the world, Austria's crime and theft rate is quite low. Nonetheless it is advisable not to leave valuable objects – especially cameras – in your car, which should always be left locked. If your passport is stolen, the police will give you a
certificate to take to your consulate.

| I want to report a theft. | **Ich möchte einen Diebstahl melden** |

CUSTOMS AND ENTRY FORMALITIES (*Zoll*)

Following are the items you can take into Austria duty-free (if you are over 17 years of age) and then back into your own country.

Into	Cigarettes		Cigars		Tobacco	Spirits		Wine
Australia	200	or	250 g.	or	250 g.	1 l.	or	1 l.
Austria 1)	200	or	50	or	250 g.	1 l.	and	2 l.
2)	400	or	100	or	500 g.	1 l.	and	2 l.
Australia	200	or	250 g.	or	250 g.	1 l.	or	1 l.
Canada	200	and	50	and	1 kg.	1.1 l.	or	1.1 l.
Eire	200	or	50	or	250 g.	1 l.	and	2 l.
N. Zealand	200	or	50	or	250 g.	1.1 l.	and	4.5 l.
S. Africa	200	and	50	and	250 g.	1 l.	and	2 l.
UK	200	or	50	or	250 g.	1 l.	and	2 l.
USA	200	and	100	and	*	1 l.	or	1 l.

1) Arriving from European countries.
2) Arriving from non-European countries.
* A reasonable quantity.

Visitors from, or returning to, other EU countries may bring unlimited quantities of the above goods bought outside duty-free shops, provided the goods are for personal use only. Tourists do not pay duty on personal jewellery, sports equipment (for personal use), gifts and souvenirs up to a value of 1000 schillings.

Currency restrictions: Foreign and Austrian money can be taken into Austria without restriction. You can export 50,000 schillings in Austrian currency and an unlimited amount of foreign currency. Banks must report transactions of 100,000 schillings or more, in line with laws aimed at preventing money-laundering.

VAT reimbursement: For purchases of more than 1,000 schillings you can have the value-added tax (*Mehrwertsteuer*) reimbursed if you are taking the goods out of the EU. The salesperson fills out a form (called 'U 34') with your home address, passport number and the amount of the purchase. At the border a customs official will stamp this form which you must then mail to the shop for reimbursement by cheque or bank-order.

I've nothing to declare.   **Ich habe nichts zu verzollen.**

It's for my personal use.   **Das ist für meinen persönlichen Gebrauch.**

D

DISABLED TRAVELLERS

Vienna has made a great effort in the domain of amenities for disabled tourists. For sightseeing programmes, contact the Vienna Tourist Board *(Wiener Fremdenverkehrsverband*, see TOURIST INFORMATION). The Board also provides information on special facilities available at hotels, restaurants, theatres, museums and other sightseeing attractions.

DRIVING IN AUSTRIA

To bring your car into Austria you will need:

- International driving licence (national licence for Europeans)
- Car registration papers
- National identity sticker for your car
- Red warning triangle in case of breakdown
- First-aid kit

120 For visitors who want to hire a car in Austria, see CAR HIRE section.

Driving regulations. Drive on the right, pass on the left. Although drivers in Austria follow the same basic rules which apply in other countries that drive on the right, some rules might differ somewhat:

- you must wear seat-belts;
- children under the age of 12 may not sit in front, and must use a special safety seat;
- on the motorway *(Autobahn)* passing another vehicle on the right is prohibited;
- vehicles coming from the right have priority at crossroads without other signals;
- trams have priority, even when coming from the left;
- vehicles must halt behind trams when they are slowing down to stop, loading or unloading passengers;
- it is prohibited to use your horn (day or night) in town;
- motorcyclists must wear crash helmets and use dipped headlights throughout the day.

Drunken driving is a very serious offence in Austria. The permissible alcohol level in the blood is 0.8 per mille.

Speed limits. On motorways (expressways) 130 kph (81 mph) or 100 kph (62 mph); on other roads 100 kph or 80 kph (50 mph); in built-up areas 50 kph (31 mph); with caravan (trailer) 80 kph on the open road; with studded tyres 100 kph on motorways, 80 kph on other roads.

Parking. In streets with tram tracks, parking is prohibited from 8 p.m. to 5 a.m. from mid-December to end March. In fact, if at all possible, you should use public transport within the Gürtel (outer ring road) since one-way streets and traffic jams add confusion within the city where there's a real lack of parking space. To park in 'blue' zones you'll need parking tickets, in use from 8 a.m. to 6 p.m. for up to 90 minutes. Tickets are available in banks and tobacco shops (Tabak-Trafik).

Breakdowns: Austrian automobile clubs offer 24-hour breakdown service to all drivers on motorways and main roads; for the ÖAMTC call 120; for the ARBÖ call 123.

Fuel and oil: There are plenty of stations, some of them self-service. In Vienna, most service stations close at night, but you can get fuel very late at highway entrances to the city.

Road signs: Most road signs employed in Austria are international pictographs but here are some written signs you might come across:

Anfang	(Parking) Start	**Ortsende**	Town ends
Ausfahrt	Exit	**Parken erlaubt**	Parking allowed
Aussicht	Viewpoint	**Rechts, links einbiegen**	Turn right, left
Bauarbeiten	Road works		
Einbahn	One way	**Rollsplitt**	Loose gravel
Ende	(Parking) End	**Sackgasse**	Dead end street
Fahrbahn- wechsel	Change lanes	**Spital**	Hospital
		Steinschlag	Falling stones
Fußgänger	Pedestrians	**Umleitung**	Diversion (detour)
Gefahr	Danger		
Geradeaus	Straight on	**Vorfahrt**	Priority
Glatteis	Slippery roads	**Vorsicht**	Caution
Halten verboten	No stopping	**Werktags von 7 bis 17 Uhr**	Weekdays 7 a.m. to 5 p.m.
Licht einschalten	Use headlights	**Zufahrt gestattet**	Entry permitted

driving licence	**Führerschein**
car registration papers	**Zulassungsschein**
green card	**Grüne Karte**
Where's the nearest car park, please?	**Wo ist der nächste Parkplatz, bitte?**
Can I park here?	**Darf ich hier parken?**
Are we on the right road for...?	**Sind wir auf der richtigen Strasse nach...**
Fill it up, please.	**Bitte volltanken.**
Check the oil/tyres/battery, please.	**Öl/Reifen/Batterie prüfen, bitte.**

I've had a breakdown.	**Ich habe eine Panne.**
There's been an accident.	**Es ist ein Unfall passiert.**

EMBASSIES and CONSULATES *(Botschaft; Konsulat)*

The following is a list of English-speaking embassies and consulates in Vienna:

Australia: Mattiellistrasse 2-4, 1040 Vienna.
Tel. 512 85 80.

Canada: Laurenzerberg 2, 1010 Vienna.
Tel. 531 38 30 00.

Eire: Landstrasser Hauptstrasse 2, 1030 Vienna.
Tel. 715 42 46 0.

New Zealand: Springsiedelgasse 28, 1090 Vienna.
Tel. 318 85 05, fax 377 66 0.

South Africa: Sandgasse 33, 1190 Vienna.
Tel. (embassy) 326 49 30; (consulate) 756 11 7.

United Kingdom: Jaurèsgasse 12, 1030 Vienna.
Tel. (embassy) 713 15 75; (consulate) 756 11 7.

USA: (embassy) Botzmanngasse 16, 1090 Vienna.
Tel. 313 39; (consulate) Gartenbaupromenade
2, 1010 Vienna. Tel. 313 39.

EMERGENCIES *(Notfälle)*

If your hotel receptionist isn't at hand, the Viennese telephone service has several emergency numbers. The most important ones are listed below. If you speak no German, try in English or find someone who speaks English to help you call. See also MEDICAL CARE.

Police emergency	133
Assistance on the road	120, 123
Fire	122
Ambulance, first aid	144
Chemist (pharmacist) on duty	15 50

| Emergency medical service | 141 |
| Emergency Dentist (nights and weekends) | 512 2078 |

I need a doctor/dentist.	**Ich brauche einen Arzt/ Zahnarzt.**
ambulance	**Krankenwagen**
Fire!	**Feuer!**
Help!	**Hilfe!**
hospital	**Spital**
police	**Polizei**

ETIQUETTE

Among themselves the Viennese have developed an elaborate system of courtesy – a left-over from the Habsburg days – in which they call one another by academic, bureaucratic and aristocratic titles, sometimes even when completely unwarranted. You will probably not get involved in this, but if you are a woman do not be surprised to hear yourself regularly addressed as Gnädige Frau (gracious lady) with the additional Küss die Hand (I kiss your hand); sometimes the hand is actually kissed for good measure! Introductions to people are always accompanied by a handshake.

When you go into a shop it is customary to say 'guten Tag' or 'Grüss Gott' (good day) or 'guten Abend' (good evening) before making your request and, of course, 'auf Wiedersehen' (goodbye) when you leave.

GETTING TO VIENNA

Although the fares and conditions described below have all been carefully checked, it is always advisable to consult a travel agent or local authority to verify the latest information on exact times, fares and other arrangements.

By Air

Scheduled flights. There is regular service to Vienna from various centres in the UK. Flying time from London is two and a half hours.

In addition to non-stop flights from New York, there is scheduled service from over 40 American cities as well as a dozen cities in Canada to European gateway destinations from which you can make connections to Vienna.

Charter flights. Cheap charter flights are readily available from the UK. Accommodation is not generally included.

Charters are scheduled from a selection of North American cities, including ABC (Advanced Booking Charter) flights good for two-, three- and four-week stays, and OTC (One-Stop Inclusive Tour Charter) package deals which include round-trip air transport, hotel accommodation, selected meals and sightseeing. In addition, dozens of American tour operators have individual and group packages to Austria offering stays of from two days to two weeks in Vienna. Consult a reputable travel agent for details of current programmes.

By Car

The quickest route to Vienna is via Ostend through Brussels, Cologne, Nuremburg, Passau and Linz, although there are more attractive routes, *die romantische Strasse*, via Rothenburg ob der Tauber, through the countryside. The ferry crossings to Ostend leave from Dover and Folkstone.

Depending on which direction you come from, you might be able to put your car on the train for part of the journey. In the summer a car-train *(Autozug)* service links Vienna with cities in Germany, Italy and former Yugoslavia. Arriving with the car-train allows you to avoid traffic jams approaching Vienna and puts you near the centre of town.

The Austrian Federal Railways runs car-trains between Vienna and Bischofshofen, Feldkirch (overnight service with couchettes also available), Lienz, Villach and Innsbruck and Salzburg (both during the skiing season only).

By Rail

The Ostend-Vienna express takes about 16 hours; the whole trip, London to Vienna, takes about 24 hours. Couchettes and sleepers are available, but must be reserved in advance.

Various special rail cards are valid for travel in Austria. The Inter-Rail Card allows unlimited travel across most of Europe and Morocco, and is available for a period of four weeks to travellers under 26. A cheaper zonal Inter-Rail Card is also available; Zone C covers Austria, Germany, Denmark and Switzerland. The Euro Domino pass is valid for unlimited travel on any 3, 5 or 10 days within a one-month period, in the country or countries of your choice.

The free Rail-Europ-Senior ticket allows pensioners 30% reduction on travel in more than 20 European countries.

Visitors from outside Europe and North Africa can buy a Eurailpass – a flat-rate, unlimited-mileage ticket good for first-class trains anywhere in western Europe, including Great Britain. Eurail Youthpass offers second-class travel at a cheaper rate to anyone under 26.

The Austrian National Railpass (Bundes-Netzkarte) entitles the holder to unlimited travel on Austrian Railways for one month. The regional 'Puzzleticket' allows four days travel on all railways during a period of ten days within one of 4 regions of Austria.

By Coach

Coach services connect London and Vienna in summer. However, overnight accommodation is usually added to the cost of the trip.

GUIDES and INTERPRETERS *(Fremdenführer; Dolmetscher)*

The most romantic tour of Vienna is the famous horse-drawn cab. These Fiaker are usually parked at the Heldenplatz, Stephanplatz or near the Albertina and will take you around the major sightseeing spots. Make sure you agree on the cost of the trip before you begin since this can vary depending on the time of day and the chosen itinerary.

Most hotels can arrange for multilingual guides or interpreters for **126** any occasion. Or you can contact:

Travel Point, Boltzmanngasse 19, 1090 Vienna. Tel. 319 42 43, fax 310 3875.

Vienna Guide Service, Sommerhaidenweg 124, 1190 Vienna. Tel. 440 3094, fax 440 2825.

We'd like an English-speaking guide.	**Wir möchten einen englisch-sprachigen Fremdenführer.**
I need an English interpreter.	**Ich brauche einen Dolmetscher für Englisch.**
How long with the ride take?	**Wie lange dauert die Fahrt?**
What does it cost?	**Was kostet es?**

LANGUAGE

Austria is, of course, German speaking, but English is also very widely understood and spoken. If you don't speak German, don't forget to ask 'Sprechen Sie Englisch?' (Do you speak English?) before plunging ahead.

The Berlitz GERMAN PHRASE BOOK AND DICTIONARY covers most situations you're likely to encounter in Austria.

Do you speak English?	**Sprechen Sie Englisch?**

LAUNDRY and DRY CLEANING

The advantage of getting your laundry washed or cleaned by the hotel is quick service, but the prices are high. Therefore it is worth seeking out neighbourhood dry-cleaners and self-service laundries. There are some laundries which do your clothes the same day. The yellow pages list addresses under 'Wäschereien'(laundries) and 'Putzereien' (dry cleaners), or your hotel receptionist will help you find the nearest establishment.

When will it be ready?	**Wann ist es fertig?**
For tomorrow morning, please.	**Bis morgen früh, bitte.**

LOST PROPERTY *(Fundamt)*

If you have mislaid or lost something you should call or go to the lost property office:

Wasagasse 22. Tel. 313 44 92 11, Monday to Friday, 8 a.m. – 12 noon.

Articles lost in trams or buses are turned in at the lost property office after 3 days (prior to that, call Vienna Transport at 790 91 05). If you have forgotten something in a taxi, try the Funk-Taxi (radio taxi) numbers. For objects lost in the train, contact the central collecting office for the Austrian Railways:

Zentralsammelstelle der Österreichischen Bundesbahnen, Langauergasse 2, Westbahnhof. Tel. 580 03 29 96.

I've lost my passport/wallet/handbag.	**Ich habe meinen Pass/meine Brieftasche/meine Handtasche verloren.**

MEDICAL CARE *(Ärztliche Hilfe)*

See also EMERGENCIES. Ask your insurance company before leaving home if medical treatment in Austria is covered by your policy.

Most chemists or drugstores (Apotheke) are open Monday to Friday and Saturday morning (see HOURS). For night and Sunday service, all chemists display the address of the nearest shop remaining on duty. To find out which chemist shops are open, tel. 15 50.

Where is there a chemist shop on duty?	**Wo is die diensthabende Apotheke?**

MONEY MATTERS *(Geld)*

See also PLANNING YOUR BUDGET, pp. 131–132. Austria's monetary unit is the Schilling, abbreviated ÖS, S or Sch., divided into Groschen (abbreviated g.). Coins come in pieces of 1, 5, 10, 20, schillings and 2, 5, 10 and 50 groschen. Be sure you don't confuse the similar 5- and 10-schilling pieces. There are banknotes of 20, 50, 100, 500 and 1,000 and, in these inflationary times, 5,000 schillings.

Banks and Currency Exchange (Bank: Wechselstube). Foreign currency can be changed in practically all banks and savings banks (Sparkasse). You can also change money at travel agencies and hotels, but the rate will not be as good. See also OPENING HOURS.

Some exchange offices are open on weekends at the airport, Südbahnhof, Westbahnhof, Air Terminal, Stephansplatz and Opern-passage. They're open from early morning (some from 6.30) until late afternoon or evening every day of the week. Note that all post offices cash Eurocheques.

Money-changing machines (CHANGE) that will take $5, $10 and $20 notes are to be found at Stephansplatz 2 (near Stephansdom), Kärntnerstrasse 32, 43 and 51, Operngasse 8 (next to the Opera), Graben 21, Michaelerplatz 3, Schottenring 1, Tegetthoffstrasse 7, Franz-Josefs-Kai 1 and Schloss Schönbrunn.

Traveller's cheques (Reisescheck) are welcome almost everywhere; but, again, the rates are best in banks or exchange offices.

I want to change some pounds/dollars.	**Ich möchte Pfund/Dollar wechseln.**
Do you accept traveller's cheques?	**Nehmen Sie Reisescheks an?**
Do you have any change, please?	**Haben Sie Kleingeld, bitte?**

NEWSPAPERS and MAGAZINES

Major hotels and most kiosks in the 1st District sell English-language daily newspapers from London, as well as the *International Herald Tribune*, *Wall Street Journal* and *USA Today*, plus the news magazines.

Monthly cultural programmes are available in the Vienna Tourist Board's *Monatsprogramm*. If you can read German and want a less formal, fresher view of the city's events, along with a full restaurant guide, we heartily recommend the monthly *Falter* magazine (similar to London's *Time Out* or New York's *Village Voice*).

OPENING HOURS

Most small shops are open from 9 a.m. (grocery stores an hour earlier)
6 p.m. with a break for lunch. Major department stores do business
from 8 a.m. to 6 p.m. non-stop, but supermarkets close for about
two hours at lunch. Shops are closed on Saturday afternoon, though
several stay open until 5 p.m. on the first Saturday of each month.
Shops in the railway stations West- and Südbahnhof are open daily
from 7 a.m. to 11 p.m.

Museum hours vary considerably, but the majority are open from
9 or 10 a.m. to 3 or 4 p.m. weekdays, and from 9 a.m. to 1 p.m. on
Saturdays and Sundays. Most are closed on Mondays.

Banks do business Mondays to Fridays from 8 a.m. to 3 p.m.
(Thursdays until 5.30 p.m.). Most branches usually close between
12.30 and 1.30 p.m.

Post offices are open Mondays to Fridays, 8 a.m. to 6 p.m. For
post offices which offer 24-hour service see section POST OFFICE.

Chemists are open from 8 a.m. to noon and from 2 p.m. to 6 p.m.;
Saturday from 8 a.m. to noon.

P

PHOTOGRAPHY

Many museums allow you to take photographs (sometimes for a
small fee) but never with a tripod or flash.

All popular film makes and sizes are available in Austria, but de-
veloping colour film may take a week or more.

I'd like a film for this camera.	**Ich möchte einen Film für diese Kamera.**
a black and white film	**ein Schwarzweissfilm**
a film for colour prints	**ein Farbfilm**
a colour-slide film	**ein Diafilm**

a 35-mm film	**ein Fünfunddreissig-Millimeter-Film**
How long will it take for this film to be developed?	**Wie lange dauert es, diesen Film zu entwickeln?**
Can I take a picture?	**Darf ich ein Foto machen?**

PLANNING YOUR BUDGET

To give you an idea of what to expect, here is a list of average prices in Austrian schillings (S). They can only be approximate, however, as in Austria, too, inflation creeps relentlessly up.

Airport. Porter 20 ÖS per bag. Bus to centre 70 ÖS, taxi 400 ÖS, train 35 ÖS.

Babysitters. 120 ÖS per hour. Minimum 3 hours, plus taxi fare.

Bicycle hire. 200–250 ÖS a day.

Car hire (advance booking from abroad, unlimited mileage, all insurance and taxes included). *VW Golf* 1,500 ÖS per day, (3-day minimum), 7,200 ÖS a week. *BMW 316* 2,400 ÖS per day (3-day minimum). *Mercedes 280E* 4,150 ÖS per day (3-day minimum), 21,000 ÖS a week.

Entertainment. Cinema 70–100 ÖS, nightclub 400–500 ÖS, disco from 50 ÖS upwards.

Guides. 1,116 ÖS for half a day, 2,232 ÖS per day.

Hotels (double room with bath per night). ***** 1,700–6,800 ÖS, **** 1,200–3,000 ÖS, *** 800–1,800 ÖS, ** 650–1,200 ÖS, * 600–1,000 ÖS. (Categories ***** and **** include breakfast.)

Meals and drinks. Continental breakfast 60 ÖS, lunch/dinner in fairly good establishment 200–300 ÖS, coffee 25–35 ÖS, Austrian wine (bottle) 200–250 ÖS, cocktail 75–100 ÖS.

Museums. Entrance fees vary considerably. Admission to municipal museums is free on Friday mornings. Concessions are available at **131**

many museums for holders of the Vienna Card. Entrance for children under six is free.

Public transport. 20 ÖS for single ticket, 17 ÖS single ticket bought in advance, 24-hour ticket 50 ÖS, 3-day ticket 113 ÖS.

Sightseeing. Fiaker 400 ÖS for a short tour, 800 ÖS for a longer one (but not that much longer!), MS Vindobona motorboat 210 ÖS.

Taxis. Meter starts at 24 ÖS, 11 ÖS per km or 4 ÖS per minute.

Tickets. Concerts 50–700 ÖS (standing 50 ÖS), opera 50–2,500 ÖS (wheelchair-places and companion 50 ÖS; standing 15–20 ÖS), Spanish Riding School training 80 ÖS, children 20 ÖS, shows 220–800 ÖS, (standing 150–160 ÖS), Vienna Boys' Choir 60–250 ÖS (standing free).

POLICE *(Polizei)*

Vienna's police wear green caps and jackets with black trousers, and drive white cars. Traffic police wear white caps and, in summer, white jackets. Street parking is supervised by 'Politessen' (metre-maids) in blue jackets and white hats. Police on motorcycles are popularly known as 'white mice' (weisse Mäuse). If you are fined for any reason, the police have the right to ask you to pay on the spot.

You can find the number of the various district police stations (Bezirkspolizeikommissariat) in the telephone book but in emergencies call 133.

Where is the nearest police station, please?	**Wo ist die nächste Polizei-Wachstube, bitte?**

POST OFFICE *(Postamt)*

Apart from the regular post office hours in most branches, the post offices at the main railway stations (Westbahnhof, Südbahnhof and Franz Josefs-Bahnhof) are open day and night, including Sundays and public holidays. Other post offices offering a 7-day-a-week 24-hour service for registered, air and express mail (with a small extra charge for after-hours service) are the following: Central Post Office, Fleischmarkt 19 and Central Telegraph Office, Börseplatz 1. For information, tel. 515 24 24.

Stamps and limited information about postage rates are also available at tobacco shops.

Mail: If you wish to receive mail by poste restante/general delivery (postlagernd), have it sent to the following address:

Hauptpostlagernd

Fleischmarkt 19

1010 Vienna, Austria

Do not forget your passport as identification when you go to pick up your mail.

Fax: many post offices have public fax services both for sending and receiving correspondence– useful if there is none at the place where you are staying. Central Post Office fax: 535 3518. If you expect to receive a fax, ask the sender to include a telephone number where you can be reached, so that the office can inform you of its arrival. (A nominal fee is charged for this latter service.)

Telegrams: The minimum for a regular telegram is 7 words. 'Night letters' (Brieftelegramm) are transmitted as a telegram and delivered to the address with the normal mail of the day. One word costs half the price of the regular telegram rate (minimum 22 words).

express (special delivery)	**Express/Eilbote**
airmail	**Luftpost**
Have you any mail for...?	**Haben Sie Post für...?**
A stamp for this letter/ post card, please.	**Eine Marke für diesen Brief /diese Postkarte, bitte.**
I want to fax a letter to...	**Ich möchte einen Brief nach... faxen.**

PUBLIC HOLIDAYS *(Feiertage)*

Austria observes 14 public holidays a year on which banks, museums, official services and many restaurants are closed. On Good Friday, a holiday for Protestants only, shops remain open.

January 1	*Neujahrstag*	New Year's Day
January 6	*Heilige Drei Könige*	Twelfth Night
May 1	*Staatsfeiertag*	Labour Day
	(Tag der Arbeit)	
August 15	*Mariä Himmelfahrt*	Assumption
October 26	*Nationalfeiertag*	National Holiday
	(Tag der Fahne)	(Flag Day)
November 1	*Allerheiligen*	All Saints' Day
December 8	*Unbefleckte*	Immaculate
	Empfängnis	Conception
December 25	*Weihnachten*	Christmas Day
December 26	*Stefanstag*	St Stephen's Day
Movable dates:	*Karfreitag*	Good Friday
	Ostermontag	Easter Monday
	Christi Himmelfahrt	Ascension Day
	Pfingstmontag	Whit Monday
	Fronleichnam	Corpus Christi

On December 24, Christmas Eve, theatres and cinemas are closed all day and shops, restaurants and coffee houses close at midday.

Are you open tomorrow?   **Haben Sie morgen geöffnet?**

PUBLIC TRANSPORT

Maps for buses, trams and the underground are available at main stops as well as at the central public transport information offices at Karlsplatz, Stephansplatz, Praterstern, Philadelphiabrücke. Weekday opening hours are 8 a.m. to 6 p.m. (Karlsplatz opens an hour earlier). Two offices – Stephansplatz and Karlsplatz – also open at weekends and on public holidays from 8.30 a.m. to 4 p.m.

Tickets can be bought from a conductor or a machine on trams and buses, from the booking office or machine for the main-line or city trains. There are different types of tickets available; the flat rate, the same for tram, train, underground (subway) travel and all bus services, is good for changes made without interruption. Discount tickets can be bought in advance from a tobacconist's (Tabak-Trafik) or the transport offices (Verkehrsbetriebe). Various travel passes are available – for 24 hours, 3 days and 8 days (or 4 days each for two people). Also worth considering is the *Vienna Card*, a 72-hour ticket costing 180 ÖS which is valid on all public transport and entitles its holder to discounts at concerts and museums.

Trams (Strassenbahn): Vienna has about 35 trams routes, making this the most important form of public transport. On most trams (and buses) the driver serves as the conductor. These vehicles carry a blue sign at the front and rear with the word Schaffnerlos ('without conductor'). If you already have a ticket, enter the tram by the door marked Entwerter and have it stamped; otherwise get in at the front and buy your ticket from the vending machine. For trams with conductors, enter at the rear to buy a ticket or have it stamped.

Buses: The airport bus service runs between the city air terminal at Landstrasser Hauptstrasse (the Hilton Hotel) and the airport every 20 or 30 minutes. The ride between the airport and the city takes about 30 minutes. The airport is also serviced by the Schnellbahn.

U-Bahn (underground/subway): Five lines operate at present, providing service to the main points in town. Tickets can be purchased from machines or ticket offices.

Schnellbahn (rapid-transit): Suburban trains depart from the Südbahnhof for certain outlying districts. The unit fare applies in the central zone, standard fares outside. Other points of departure are Wien Nord and Wien Mitte.

R

RADIO and TV
Room TVs in many Vienna hotels now carry English-language satellite and cable stations. Vienna radio carries daily English-language

news programmes. BBC World Service shortwave radio programmes are available on 9410 kHz.

RELIGIOUS SERVICES

Austria is predominantly Roman Catholic, but a good number of other denominations and faiths hold services regularly. Sunday mass in some churches is accompanied by orchestral and choral works. Consult a newspaper under Kirchenmusik for exact times, especially on Sundays or religious holidays.

An English-language Catholic mass is held at 5.15 p.m. at the Deutsch ordenskirche, Singerstrasse 7. There is an Anglican/ Episcopal Church at Jaurèsgasse 17–19.

Jewish services take place at the Stadttempel, Seitenstettengasse 4, for prayer times. Tel. 531 04.

TAXIS *(Taxi)*

Vienna's taxis can be caught directly at a rank, at busy locations throughout Vienna (such as at the main railway stations), or you can hail one in the street. There are never enough taxis at rush hour, so it would be wise to book in advance through your hotel receptionist or by calling one of the following numbers:

Tel. 31 300; 40 100; 60 160; or 91 011.

If you want to go beyond the city limits the fare should be discussed beforehand.

TELEPHONES *(Fernsprecher)*

Glass-enclosed grey metallic booths are scattered throughout the city. They can be recognized by a sign with a black receiver in a yellow circle on the door, and the word Fernsprecher.

The booths all have multilingual instructions. All phone boxes are equipped for long-distance calls. All calls are cheaper from 6 p.m. to 8 a.m. and on Saturdays, Sundays and Public Holidays. Note that on certain old-style telephones, a red button has to be pressed for connection the moment your party answers.

Surcharges on long-distance calls made from hotels are high. To keep costs down, go to the nearest post office or use any suitable public payphone, especially for calls abroad. Anyone telephoning a lot should obtain a pre-paid card (Wertkarte) from a post office.

Information operator for Austria:	16 11
Information operator for Germany	16 12
Information operator for the rest of Europe	16 13
Information operator for the rest of the world	16 14
Operator for abroad (to reverse charges):	09

TICKETS *(Karten)*

Tickets for performances can be obtained at private ticket agencies (Theaterkartenbüro) all over the city, as well as at major hotels, but these will cost at least 22 per cent more. Try Vienna Ticket Service, 1043 Vienna, Postfach 160. Tel. 587 98 43, fax 587 98 44.

Concerts. Tickets are usually sold by subscription, and are rarely available at the box office or by post. To book the occasional seat on sale to the public contact:

Wiener Philharmoniker, Bösendorferstrasse 12, 1010 Vienna (often sold out) Musikalische Jugend, same address as above.

Spanish Riding School. Written orders for tickets are essential and should be sent at least six months in advance to: Spanische Reitschule, Hofburg, 1010 Vienna. Tickets can be bought on the day for the morning training sessions.

Opera and Theatre. The best place for opera tickets is the national theatre ticket office (Österreichischer Bundestheaterverband, Bestellbüro). They sell tickets seven days ahead for opera (Staatsoper), operetta (Volksoper), Burgtheater and Akademietheater performances (closed in July and August); you can reserve tickets at least 3 weeks before the performance by writing to the same address:

Bundestheaterkassen, Goethegasse 1, 1010 Vienna. For information the number to call is 514 44 29 59 or 514 44 29 60. Ticket sales by **137** credit card are available six days in advance. Tel. 513 1513 or fax 514 44 2969.

Vienna Boys' Choir (Wiener Sängerknaben). Obtain tickets in advance at the Hofburg Kapelle on Fridays from 5 to 7 p.m. for Sunday performances, or reserve at least two months in advance from:

Hofmusikkapelle, Hofburg, Schweizerhof, 1010 Vienna.

The choir can also be heard every Friday at the Konzerthaus in May, June, September and October. Tickets are available from major hotels, or Reisebüro Mondial, Faulmanngasse 4, 1040 Vienna.

TIME DIFFERENCES

Austria follows Central European Time (GMT+1). In summer, clocks move ahead one hour, and the time difference looks like this:

New York	London	**Vienna**	Jo'burg	Sydney	Auckland
6 a.m.	11 a.m.	**noon**	noon	8 p.m.	10 p.m.

TIPPING

Since a service charge is included in hotel and restaurant bills, tipping is not obligatory. However, it's appropriate to give something extra to porters, cloakroom attendants, etc., for their services. The chart below makes some suggestions as to how much to leave.

Hotel porter, per bag	20 ÖS
Maid, per week	50 ÖS
Waiter	5% (optional)
Lavatory attendant	10 ÖS
Taxi driver	round off fare
Tour guide	10%
Barber/Hairdresser	10-15%
Theatre usher	10 ÖS

TOILETS (Toiletten)

Public facilities can be found near important streets or squares, often in the pedestrian underpasses. Normally toilets in cafés can be used without ordering anything but it's always more courteous to have a coffee or a beer. If hand towels and soap are used, there is often a set fee rather than just tip. Have a couple of schillings ready in case the door has a 'slot' machine.

Toilets may be labelled with symbols of a man and a women, the initials WC, or with Damen (Ladies) and Herren (Gentlemen).

TOURIST INFORMATION

The Austrian National Tourist Office (Österreichische Fremden-verkehrswerbung), a non-commercial organization (which cannot make reservations), has representatives in many countries (see list below). They can inform you about what to see, when to go and where to stay in and around Vienna:

Australia: ANTO, 1st Floor, 36 Carrington Street, Sydney NSW 2000. Tel. (2) 299-3621, fax 299-3808.

Canada: ANTO, 2 Bloor Street East, Suite 3330, Toronto, Ontario M4W 1A8. Tel. (416) 967-3381, fax 967-4101.

Eire: ANTO, Merrion Hall, Strand Road, Sandymount, PO Box 2506, Dublin 4. Tel. (01) 283-0488, fax 283-0531.

Great Britain: ANTO, 30 St. George Street, London W1R OAL. Tel. (0171) 629-0461, fax (0171) 499-6038.

South Africa: ANTO, Cradock Heights, 21 Cradock Avenue, Rosebank, 2196 Johannesburg. Tel. (11) 442-7235, fax 442-8304.

USA: ANTO, PO Box 1142, New York, NY 10108-1142. Tel. (212) 944-6880, fax 730-4568.

ANTO, PO Box 491938, Los Angeles, CA 90049. Tel. (310) 477-3332, fax (310) 477-5141.

Or get in touch with the **Vienna Tourist Board**:
(Wiener Fremdenverkehrsverband), Obere Augartenstrasse 40, 1025 Vienna. Tel. (1) 211 140, fax 216 8492, Monday to Friday 8 a.m. to 4 p.m.; Kärntnerstrasse 38, 1010 Vienna. Tel. 513 88 92, seven days a week 9 a.m. to 7 p.m.

Bureaus are also located in the Opernpassage (pedestrian subway near the Opera), in the Westbahnhof and Südbahnhof and at the airport.

Austria Information Centre (Österreich-Information): Margaretenstrasse 1, 1040 Vienna. Tel. 587 2000.

TRAINS *(Zug)*

The main railway stations in Vienna are the Westbahnhof (connections with the western part of Austria, Germany and Switzerland), the Südbahnhof (for links with southern Austria, Hungary, the Balkans and Italy) and the Franz-Josefs-Bahnhof (connections with north and northwest Austria, Czech and Slovak Republics).

Tickets can be purchased and reservations made in travel agencies or at the railway stations. Reductions are available in certain cases and children under six travel free. For all train information, phone 1717 (employees are both knowledgeable and helpful). The following is a description of the types of trains found in Austria:

Expresszug	1st and 2nd class, the fastest trains
Schnellzug/ Städteschnellzug	The biggest towns in Austria are connected by these very fast, convenient trains, which leave Vienna every two hours from 7 a.m.
Eilzug	1st and 2nd class; make a number of local stops
Personenzug	local trains which stop at almost every station

Schlafwagen	**Speisewagen**	**Liegewagen**
Sleeping car with 1-, 2- or 3-bed compartments including washing facilities.	Dining-car	Sleeping-berth car (couchette) with blankets, sheets and pillows.

When's the best/ next train to...?	**Wann fährt der günstigste/ nächste Zug nach...?**
single (one-way)	**einfach**
return (round-trip)	**hin und zurück**
first/second class	**erste/zweite Klasse**

I'd like to make a seat reservation.	**Ich möchte einen Platz reservieren.**

WATER *(Wasser)*

Viennese water, which comes from the Styrian Alps, tastes mountain-fresh, so for the time being the Viennese don't have to worry about making a distinction between tap water and drinking water. If you come across a sign Kein Trinkwasser, however, the water is not fit for drinking.

YOUTH HOSTELS *(Jugendherberge)*

There is a large, modern hostel near the Danube as you enter Vienna from the north with two and four beds to a room. You can obtain a map and information there about the other 100 hostels in Austria.

Austrian Youth Hostels Association, Gonzagagasse 22 (Schottenring), 1010 Vienna. Tel. 533 53 53.

Jugendgästehaus, Friedrich-Engelsplatz 24, 1200 Vienna, Austria. Tel. 332 82 94, 330 05 98, fax 330 8379.

Index

144